ANNA AND BENT

Adventurers for God

by Bent Axel Larsen

PACIFIC PRESS PUBLISHING ASSOCIATION
Mountain View, California
Omaha, Nebraska
Oshawa, Ontario

Library of Congress Catalog Card No. 79-83894

Contents

1

Anna's Call and Decision

During the school year of 1927 excitement stirred the "White City," as the great Skodsborg Sanitarium near Copenhagen, Denmark, is called. A noted missionary family had arrived. There would be a meeting that evening. The missionary would tell experiences from his work among the natives of Peru. Missionaries often came to visit Skodsborg. But this time someone special came, not as usual from some Northern European mission field in Africa, but from the land of the Incas in South America. And what a missionary—a tall, broad, robust man.

"There he comes," voices whispered as he entered the auditorium. Every head turned to see missionary F. A. Stahl walking down the aisle with his wife and their little adopted tattooed Indian girl from the Amazon jungle. What a stirring message! What thrilling experiences! What an irresistible appeal! The students from nearby Naerum Mission School and many young people at the sanitarium found their enthusiasm for missions kindled as never before.

The little, adopted, once-heathen girl sang as a testimony of what the gospel had done for her and for her people. No one understood the words, sung in Spanish, but her clear, sweet voice made a deep impression on many hearts.

The Stahls remained longer at Skodsborg than at any other place on their European tour. Elder Stahl was of German descent, and Mrs. Stahl of Swedish. And to the delight of all she spoke Swedish. The Stahls conducted many meetings at Skodsborg and at the school, as well as throughout Scandinavia. Their tremendous influence among young people inspired almost everyone to want to go to South America as a missionary. Even the conference president said he thought seriously of going.

One afternoon the language teacher, Mrs. Ingeborg Hjartarson, was talking with Anna Jensen, a senior student. "I have to go down to the sanitarium to visit the Stahls," she said. "Would you like to go with me?"

"Would I? I would love to!" Anna jumped up and slammed shut the book she had been reading. With her, as with most of her comrades, there were few things she would rather do than have the privilege of meeting Elder and Mrs. Stahl personally. "I shall be ready in a few minutes," she said.

On the two-mile walk through the beautiful Skodsborg forest they discussed the meetings and the rewards of mission service. Even under a gray sky, somehow the teacher's enthusiastic words seemed to warm Anna's heart like the brightest sunshine. It seemed that all the students loved Mrs. Hjartarson. Her radiant personality, her helpful disposition, and her enthusiasm for missions inspired the young people. Many a missionary, looking back, finds that he owes to her his first encouragement to enter mission service. In the day when God bestows His rewards, surely stars will bejewel her crown for souls won in far-off lands.

At the missionaries' room in the sanitarium Mrs. Hjartarson introduced Anna to the Stahl family. They spoke in German. Anna tried her best to catch a word now and then. After a long while, Elder Stahl said, "*Wir wollen beten.*" And they all knelt while the missionary and Mrs. Hjartarson both prayed in German.

Anna had not been able to follow the conversation, but she had the impression that much had been said about her. During the prayers she felt the moving of the Holy Spirit. Her heart went up to God in earnest surrender and praise.

Mrs. Stahl embraced Anna in good South American style and said in Swedish, "God bless you Anna. I love you." She smiled at her. "I am also Ana, you know. We will like one another," she said.

The sweet smile she got from Mrs. Stahl made Anna happy. She made a curtsy—young Scandinavian style—shook her hand and smiled back.

Pastor Stahl also shook Anna's hand vigorously. "*Auf Wiedersehen,*" he said.

"*Auf Wiedersehen,*" Anna repeated. She knew that much German.

While they walked through the picturesque Skodsborg forest, Anna had a feeling that, for her, something wonderful had taken place in the sanitarium room. The sun suddenly burst its warm rays through an opening in the clouds and painted lovely spots of wild flower beds under the tender-budded trees. The air smelled wonderfully of spring freshness. The birds seemed never to have sung more cheerfully.

8

"Did you understand what we were talking about with the Stahls?" asked Mrs. Hjartarson.

"No. I am sorry." Anna, full of eager curiosity, looked at her teacher. "I really did not understand much. But I had the impression that you talked a whole lot about me."

"We did." Mrs. Hjartarson seemed to hesitate a little. "I wanted them to know you really well. So I told them everything I knew about you."

"Why?" Anna asked in wonder.

"You see, Anna, the Stahls want you to go with them to South America."

"South America!" Anna exclaimed, "When?"

"Oh, in about a month."

Anna stood motionless on the footpath they had followed beside the main road. She felt as though a bomb had exploded right behind her. When she had recuperated a little from the shock, she stammered: "A month! You mean to say that—that I—that I shall go with—with the Stahls—to Peru—within a month?"

"Yes. You have been wanting to go out as a missionary, haven't you? Here is your opportunity. You are willing to go, aren't you?"

The question was like another bomb blast. How could she answer? "But, this is so sudden!" she said.

"You have heard the wonderful, thrilling experiences the missionaries have told. You will soon be right in the middle of them. You will be a missionary!" Mrs. Hjartarson's voice vibrated with enthusiasm.

Yes, she had wanted to be a missionary. It had been her dream. She had prepared herself for it, longed and prayed for it. But now the thought overwhelmed her. How could she, all alone, a young girl, venture halfway round the world to give her life for the people in the Peruvian jungles?

"But how can I?" she asked. "How can I go so soon, all alone, that far away from all my friends and relatives?"

"You won't be alone." Mrs. Hjartarson understood. She put her arm around Anna's shoulders and held her tight. "You will be like a daughter of that wonderful missionary family. You know how much God has blessed Elder Stahl as the great, modern apostle to the highland Inca Indians. Their experiences will be yours and their blessings will be your blessings. What you learn, being with them, will be a great help to you as a future missionary."

Anna looked up through the delicate, light-green foliage into the blue sky. "I know that will be a great privilege."

"Sister Stahl needs you. She wants you to be her companion while her husband makes his long trips out among the native villages. You can be a great help to her. She loves you."

Anna's eyes looked away again—far off into the lofty green-bordered sky. In her mind one thing was sure: she wanted to follow her Saviour. "If it is God's will that I shall go," she said, "I will not hesitate. I will go."

Mrs. Hjartarson never showed the slightest doubt that God had called Anna to go with the Stahls. "God has marvelously opened the way for you to become a missionary. He has called you to serve in His vineyard as a messenger of love to the people in the far-off regions of the great Amazon."

Anna's heart was still torn between two tremendous thoughts: the sudden call to sacrifice all for the Lord and the awesome privilege that had come to her. Among all her fellow students and the many eager, well-prepared young people at the sanitarium she had been chosen to go with the Stahls to the land of the Incas. She could not quite get over it. But as they continued walking in silence in the beauty of the spring afternoon, Anna felt the nearness of God. Her young heart beat with joy and thankfulness. God had called her! She would become a missionary to South America!

When the news broke, it ran like wildfire through the school and the sanitarium. "Anna Jensen is going to South America with Elder and Mrs. Stahl!"

The enthusiasm gripped all. It gave the young people a certain satisfaction to know that one of their own would be out there in that interesting mission territory of Peru. Anna became very popular. People everywhere congratulated her and showed their interest in helping. But it was not until then that she fully realized how much she must give up. She knew it would not be easy. But she had never dreamed it would be that hard. Hers was not a formal call. She would have to pay her own way. She would not receive salary, and she had no promise for the future, no furloughs, not even a guarantee for the return trip.

In her room at the school Anna sat thinking of these problems. She had given her promise to the Stahls and expressed her joy and appreciation for the privilege of going with them. She had discussed it with Mrs. Hjartarson, who had encouraged her and filled her with optimism. "We will get the money. Don't worry."

Anna had confidence in her teacher, and she believed in God. She felt sure that somehow everything would come out all right. And still—

"Do you know what they're saying about you?" Her roommate Ruth cried, bursting into the room.

"No."

"They say you are crazy!"

"Oh, it doesn't feel so bad to be crazy."

"Seriously. I overheard a conversation about you down the hall. Some students were talking with faculty members. They really think you are crazy to go like that—entirely at your own expense with neither the church nor the conference having anything to do with it. You would have no salary. It would be impossible for you to get ready in two weeks when the Stahls are leaving. And you will never be able to raise the amount of money it will cost you for such a long trip."

"Oh, Anna," Ruth continued earnestly, "are you really sure that it's God's will? Why don't you just let it pass? It seems so impossible."

Anna knew her roommate well. She loved her. They were intimate friends. "I know you love me, Ruth." Anna looked up from the letter she was trying to write to her father. "You want the very best for me. You have been so enthusiastic about my going, and it is thoughtful of you to want me to stay with you."

"But, Anna, another thing they said—they will not let you graduate!"

"They will. Mrs. Hjartarson and I talked with P. A. (the principal of the school, P. A. Christiansen). He assured us it would be worked out. I will only miss a couple weeks, you know."

"Oh, but how can you be ready so soon?"

"The Stahls are leaving here. But they have many other appointments and will stay in England for some time. I will meet them there and join them on their trip to New York."

"But—oh, Anna!" Ruth was still openly upset. "Your family—what will they say when they hear that you are going just like that, without any guarantee?"

"I am just writing my father. He has always wanted me to be a missionary. He will understand." (Her mother had died years ago when Anna was only a young girl.)

"And the money—where will you ever get that much?"

"Mrs. Hjartarson is helping me. She is wonderful. She is asking everybody to help. And she is also selling many of my things for me. She gets good prices for them."

"You are selling all your things?"

"Everything."

"Your good sewing machine? You told me how long you had saved and how hard you worked to be able to buy it. And your brand-new bicycle?"

"Yes, everything has to go. I have some jewels—rings and pins and earrings from the time before I became an Adventist. They are worth something. And my fancy fur coat." Anna held the fountain pen to her mouth and looked thoughtfully out of the window. "How I loved that coat. It was quite expensive. My aunt helped me get it. It is very nice, but not for a missionary, especially not in the Amazon jungles."

With a rap on the door Erna, a fellow student, stuck her head in. "P. G. wants to talk to you, Anna, in the faculty office." She put her hand over her mouth and blinked. "He is going to tell you not to go to South America."

Elder P. G. Nielsen, her beloved Bible teacher, was waiting for Anna in the office.

"I hear that you are going to South America," he began.

"Yes. Isn't it wonderful how God has opened the way? I'll be a missionary!"

"I don't want to discourage you, Miss Jensen. But I have been thinking about you and your plans, and I cannot but wonder if this is really God's will. Are you certain you should go without the protection of our organization?"

"I am sure it's God's will," Anna blurted out with such assurance and confidence that even her teacher, who knew her so well, expressed surprise.

"Now, Miss Jensen, what makes you so absolutely sure?"

"A call from God is something," Anna hesitated, "something that a person experiences. Isn't it? Something like a conversion? You cannot explain it, but you know it is real."

"Yes, that is right. But you must be sure. One may be mistaken, you know. God's church has an organization, and when He calls a young person to His service, He does it through the organization—through the mission board."

"I know," Anna said humbly and bowed her head. "But God has many ways. A mission board may also make a mistake and call a wrong person. But when God calls, He makes no mistakes." Then she said firmly, "I have promised Elder and Mrs. Stahl. And with God's help I will go."

"You seem very sure, Miss Jensen. May God bless you. You know that I wish only the very best for you. Let me tell you this, though: It is not good for young lovers to be separated so far from each other."

The Bible teacher had probed the one spot in Anna's heart which she could not bear to have touched. She knew he referred to her love for a fellow student, Bent Larsen. She had promised to marry Bent. How could she say good-bye to her sweetheart? How could she leave him and go so far away?

"I can only say that if God does not want me to go, He will surely and clearly prevent me."

"He will," said Elder Nielsen.

Shaken over the conversation, although she did not show it, Anna left the office with these words, "It is not good for young lovers to be separated so far from each other," still burning inside her. "He really knows how to play on heartstrings, doesn't he?" she thought. In the library she found her friend, Bent, one who never had doubted the divine leading in her plans or even suggested that she should stay home or wait, even though her departure was just as painful for him as for her.

2

Help From the Lord

Anna had made her decision. Now she acted accordingly. The preparations for her trip had to be made quickly. Many, many things had to be attended to. Her room—what a busy place! A special wardrobe for the jungle climate had to be sewn. Mrs. Christiansen, the principal's wife, brought her sewing machine over and, together with others, helped sew dresses for Anna of thin material for the tropics.

One fellow student, Carl Ilsgaard, a tailor and son of a tailor, sewed her a nice suit. A friend made a special tin-covered suitcase, almost air-tight to keep out ants and other insects.

All her friends showed their interest and their willingness to help. Maps, travel logs, passport, gifts, vaccination certificates, suitcases, and books on South America occupied her room, her time, and her mind. She seemed already to be in South America. Everything cost money. All she owned had been sold—even her hope chest of linen sheets and embroidered tablecloths and other items every young Scandinavian girl wants to have ready for her wedding day. Although many had helped, she still lacked enough money to buy a ticket.

"Hello, Miss Jensen, I want to express my best wishes for your mission adventure," the conference president spoke to her one day at the school entrance.

"Thank you, Elder Resen," Anna smiled. "I feared that you might be opposed."

"No, not really. We had hoped that you would be a worker for us here in our conference. But now that it is clear you are really going to Peru, we sincerely wish you God's blessings."

"I appreciate your encouragement. I shall do my utmost to represent my home conference and my country in the very best way."

"I am sure you will. The Inca Union is a very interesting and needy mission field. I wish I could go there myself. But I will have to stay. I can assure you of this, however—had you waited a little, you would have received a call to serve as a missionary in our own European Division. It would be much more secure for you, you know."

Should she have waited? Sometimes her friends' good arguments for not going seemed to overwhelm her. But if it was God's call, she dared not disobey. And if not, it would be up to Him to prevent her going. She had only one fervent desire—to know for sure that this *was* the will of God. She spent many hours in prayer about it. Bent also prayed far into the night.

One night while in earnest prayer, Anna asked the Lord for a sign. "You know, Lord," she said, "that my only desire is to do Your will. I have given my life and all to You. You know also that I need more money to pay for my trip. If it is Your will that I should go to Peru, send me the sum of money I need—500 crowns—as a gift, without my asking anyone for it." Then she believed that God had answered her prayer.

One May afternoon Anna and Bent met under the trees just behind the school. The birches were beginning to turn green. The spring sun shone through the exquisite foliage on thousands of blooming anemones that covered the ground. In the wonderful, beautiful springtime the two lovers stood talking. From a photographer Anna had brought some sample pictures for friends and for her passport. As they stood there choosing the best picture, Anna suddenly felt a sharp pain in her right leg. "Oh," she screamed, "it bit me! A dog bit me!"

The animal had sneaked up behind them and without even a warning bark had bitten deeply into Anna's leg. It was not a large dog, but it had an ugly look, and its mouth foamed and slavered.

"Wasn't that a strange dog?" Anna asked later when she had received proper care at the sanitarium. "It bit so hard and just stood there with a mean expression, as if it were saying, 'There you are, now! You *cannot* go to South America after all!' "

The sanitarium cared for Anna well. The physicians did everything they could to speed her recovery. During her several days in bed everyone showed her special kindnesses. And although the sign on the door said, "Please do not disturb," Bent had a standing permit to enter.

Anna sat up in bed one afternoon. She did not feel sick. Her leg—almost healed—did not hurt. "I ought to be up and out of here getting ready for my trip," she thought. However, she felt happy and thankful to God for this quiet, restful time that had come to her right in the middle of the most agitated days of her life. Surely God must have seen what was best for her.

Sunshine filled the room. Anna could look out on the flower-filled sanitarium garden across the busy highway, out over the lovely, still waters of Øresund, just beyond, where white sails dotted the tree-bordered blue.

A nurse quietly opened the door and smiled , and then opened the door wider. A small broad-shouldered man appeared.

"Why, hello, Daddy! What a wonderful surprise to see you here." Anna felt so glad to see her father that she almost jumped out of bed.

"How are you, my Anna girl? I received your letter and heard about your trouble. So I came to see you."

From a devout Lutheran family of eight children only Anna had become an Adventist. Her parents had enjoyed the respect of all their neighbors. They were known as sincere Christians. Her father was a popular lay preacher. They had experienced the joy of seeing all of their children, one by one, give their hearts to the Lord and enjoy a genuine conversion. But with Anna it had been different. Although she had always shown interest in religious services, in hymn singing and worship, she had never shown the marked conversion experience her sisters and brothers enjoyed.

Often her father and mother had had revival meetings in their home. All neighbors from miles around were invited. A visiting preacher would expound the Word of God, and her father would also give a speech or tell a heart-touching story. These had been occasions of much spiritual joy in which everyone felt drawn close to God. They would also serve coffee with cakes and cookies. A happy Christian fellowship had prevailed.

One day after one such revival meeting, a sincere

Christian asked in a friendly voice, "Are you at peace with God, dear Anna?"

Anna could not answer. She liked church and Sunday School, but she had not been troubled over her sins.

Concerned over her, the good neighbor had spoken to her mother.

"We must have patience," her mother had said. "God has His time and His ways. When it is God's time, Anna will have her own experience with her Saviour."

She did. But not until she one day accidently attended an Adventist evangelistic meeting. While she worked and studied in the capital city, Copenhagen, she sang in the choir of one of the most famous churches in the city and heard the sermons of one of Denmark's greatest preachers every Sunday. On a Sunday afternoon, coming out of a theatrical performance with some of her friends of the choir, she noticed a sign on a nearby auditorium announcing a Bible lecture on the prophecies of Daniel.

"Let us go in there," she suggested, "just for fun, and hear what he has to say." Anna had always wondered about the meaning of the prophetic symbols of animals, horns, etc., in Revelation.

They attended the meeting. It became the turning point in Anna's religious life—the beginning of a meaningful, purposeful and happy life for her. However, for her faithful Lutheran father it was not a happy turn of events. He believed with all sincerity that his daughter had gone astray. When she joyfully came home and told with fervent eagerness about her wonderful experiences with the Lord and her newfound truth, her father sadly said, "It is like a sword has gone through my soul. It would almost have been better if you had died." He loved Anna, and yet, with a pale face and trembling voice, he told her to go and not come home anymore.

Although his hard attitude toward his daughter had softened somewhat since that time, he still worried over her religion. Now she wanted to venture out, entirely on her own, to the other end of the world!

"My dear Anna girl, listen to your father. It makes me very glad to know you want to go out as a missionary, but not like that. You should not travel on your own responsibility. How can I permit you to go that way?"

"You will let me go if it is God's will, won't you?" she pleaded.

"Yes, my girl. We must always obey God's calling. But is this from God? I have been informed that you will not receive any salary or have any security in case of sickness or emergency. What will you do if you get sick?"

"God will be with me. He has promised that. He will help me. You believe that, Father. Should I not always trust in God?"

"It would break my heart should something happen to you so far away. You must also think of your loved ones at home. We would feel so much better if you were sent as other missionaries, at the responsibility of a church or a mission board."

"I trust in the Lord, Father. I am sure He has called me. But if He shows me that I should not go, I promise I shall stay and come right home to visit you. You will pray for me, won't you?"

"Yes, Anna dear, I certainly will." Her father looked at her with much love in his eyes. "You know how much we will miss you."

Anna had always looked up to her father as a man of God. She could not help being impressed by his sincere warning. She cried as she kissed him good-bye and for long after as she sat thinking the situation over and over again. Could it all be a mistake? God had not given her the sign, the money she had so earnestly asked Him for. Did this experience really mean she should not go? No, somehow she felt she should yet wait on God.

Next morning Elder Nielsen came to visit her.

"Don't you see, Miss Jensen, that it is God's finger?" He shook his long forefinger right at her. "God had to send a dog to bite you to show that you should not go to Peru."

Anna loved and respected her Bible teacher. "Maybe you are right, Elder Nielsen," she said quietly.

"Maybe! How can you doubt it? Didn't you say that God would prevent it if it was not His will? And now you are here and cannot go."

"Yes, I can go. There is still time. The Lord has just given me a few days of rest here. I believe He will show me His sign."

"His sign?" The teacher looked surprised.

"Yes. I have not told this to anyone, but I prayed to God for a sign. I asked Him to give me 500 crowns, not from any friend or by begging, but as a gift from Him."

Elder Nielsen knew Anna's sincerity. He did not want to discourage her faith. "God bless you, Miss Jensen," he said. "You will never trust God in vain. If it pleases Him, He will give you His sign."

A knock sounded on the door. A tall, handsome, elderly gentleman came in—Mr. C. Hansen, general manager of the sanitarium.

"Hello, Miss Jensen." He smiled.

"How are you, Elder Nielsen?"

The pastor nodded politely. "Very well, thank you."

"I have good news for the dog-bitten girl." Mr. Hansen handed an envelope to Anna. "Here is a check for you."

"A check! For me!"

"Yes, a check from the dog."

"From the dog! You are joking, Mr. Hansen."

"The owner had him insured. And now the insurance company sends you a check for the damages he caused you."

"Oh, thank you!" Anna opened the envelope in a hurry. "What? Five hundred and seventy-eight crowns! That is seventy-eight crowns more than I asked the Lord for!" She held the check triumphantly up before her teacher. "You see, Elder Nielsen, God wants me to go to South America."

"He does," said director Hansen. "The sanitarium has been pleased to help you and we wish you Heaven's best blessings."

"Oh, how can I ever be thankful enough? I owe so much to this wonderful institution." Her eyes filled with tears of joy and gratefulness.

Now there could be no more doubt. God had willed that she should go to South America.

3

Anna's Journey With the Stahl Family

In London the Stahls and the mission board's travel agent met Anna when she came on the train from the port of Harwich. Passport examination, baggage and customs over with, they went through the great city out to Stanborough Missionary College in Stanborough Park, Watford, about ten miles from London, where the Stahls had already been guests for some time.

How marvelously interesting to come to a foreign country, Anna thought. She sincerely appreciated the kindness and friendliness everybody showed her though she still could not help feeling a little lonesome and lost among strange people of whose language she understood but little. But this feeling vanished at the college, when one of the girls, in the room she was to share with three others, greeted her in Danish.

"How do you do, Anna Jensen. Welcome to Stanborough!"

Anna felt delighted and surprised. She looked at the

friendly greeter, and now she remembered. "Oh yes, you are Miss Belle Nielsen. Am I glad to see you, and especially to hear you! Isn't it an awful experience not to understand what people say?"

They had not been friends, had just known one another by name. But now in an instant they were close friends. They talked and talked. They knew their two roommates could not understand, and they did not want to disturb them. So they crawled into one bed and lay there whispering and giggling.

"Did you enjoy the trip over here?"

"I'll say I did! There is something exciting about traveling alone and seeing new places and people. But the language—I thought I knew a lot of English, and now I find I don't."

"Don't I know. I went through the same experience last year. Terrible! But now I speak pretty good English. It won't take you long. Tell me about the trip."

"Well, on the train and ferries through Denmark I had an enjoyable time. But I felt terribly sick all the way on the boat over the North Sea."

"Everyone gets sick. The North Sea is always rough. I felt so sick I thought I would die. Did you come right from Copenhagen?"

"No, I came from Nyborg, Bennie's hometown on Funen."

"Who is Bennie?"

"Bent Larsen, my fiancé. He came with me to Nyborg."

"I don't know him. He must be a nice fellow. How do you dare to leave him like that and go all the way to South America?"

"Oh, not easily. But I have to try him out. If he loves me—and he does—he will come after me."

"Are you sure?"

"Yes, sure. He is going to the United States to study and will later come to Peru."

"Wonderful!"

And so they whispered almost all the night through.

A week in England passed like a flash, with trips to the great city, its museums, and other places of interest. There were visits to Stanborough Press and the sanitarium and Granose Foods factory in Watford. She was also keeping up with Elder Stahl's busy speaking schedule. Then came the big day when Anna had to say good-bye to her new friends at Stanborough College. Miss Belle Nielsen soon afterward received a call to Kenya as a missionary, and Anna traveled with the Stahls to Southampton to board the world's greatest passenger liner, the gigantic SS *Leviathan.*

What a thrilling experience for Anna! On the boat she and the Stahls' adopted Indian daughter made many friends among the passengers. She made full use of the opportunity to practice her English. Full of love for God and His message, Anna found many opportunities to witness for Him. The Stahls were a great inspiration to her. Already on this first trip with them she learned valuable lessons from their consecrated lives and characters. Elder Stahl had two big meetings on the boat in which he told mission experiences and had little Chavi in her native costumes as a living illustration.

New York! What a city! What a tremendous experience, arriving in the greatest harbor in the world! What a thrill to view the Statue of Liberty from the top deck of the great *Leviathan*! What excitement docking, and what turmoil getting through immigration, customs, etc.! And, oh, what traffic! What buildings! Anna felt overwhelmed.

The month they spent in the huge metropolis passed

like an exciting dream. Mr. Adolph Dorn, the transportation agent, had arranged for their stay in the city. He met them at the dock. He knew all the best shopping opportunities, and for sight-seeing there could not have been a better guide. His able, helpful secretary, Miss Mabel Porter, and Anna became very good friends.

Almost every night Elder Stahl had a speaking engagement someplace or other. Several times they took the wrong train at the subway station or they got off at the wrong stop. One evening they were a whole hour late to an important meeting.

In the exciting month of June 1927, Charles Lindberg made his historic solo flight over the Atlantic Ocean. When he came back New York went wild. The Stahls and Anna were right in the middle of the celebration. It all made an unforgettable impression on Anna.

To her friends in the young people's societies in Denmark Anna wrote the following letter about her trip to South America: "Dear friends: When I think of the experiences I had on the trip from Denmark to Iquitos in Peru, I recall the prophecies concerning what will take place in the last days. In a striking way we see fulfilled what God's servants foretold hundreds of years ago. Only little does one realize what the world is like, when living in peaceful little Denmark. We think that the lawlessness is great there, but when one travels in other lands he sees and hears things he never dreamed of, and this is especially true in South America.

"To go into detail about my stay in England and in New York will occupy too much space. Our one-month stay in New York went by very rapidly. Elder Stahl had many meetings, and everywhere our people showed great interest in his work in Peru. I met many good Danish friends and believers at the meetings. Then we traveled again for three weeks by boat in order to get to Lima in Peru. There the Stahls had a little house; but it had to be sold, and this could not easily be done, humanly speaking. However the Stahls knew who could help them with their worries. Three times a day at our worship we prayed a special prayer to God, that He would help Brother Stahl to sell everything they had. . . .

"During our stay in Lima, Mrs. Stahl became ill with malaria. She suffered much with high fever, but at one time she sat up in her bed and said aloud, 'Yes, the evil one will not allow that I shall go to Iquitos and work for the Lord; but even if I should die on the way I will show God that I am willing to go, when He calls me.'

"Lima is a beautiful city, and especially Miraflores (look at flowers), a suburb where the missionaries live and where our industrial school is located. The many gardens and the breeze from the Pacific Ocean give it a pleasant freshness.

"Many rich people live here in great mansions. They are the landowners; the cotton producers; the cattle, sheep, llama and alpaca ranchers; and the mine owners, who have exploited the cheap labor of the poor people. In contrast most people are extremely poor.

"Mrs. Stahl and I went visiting the sick, and greater poverty I have never seen: dirty, ragged, sick people who live in shacks with no floor and no windows; and, as a whole, these people have many children.

"If one asks about the father to these children, the answer might well be that no two of them have the same father. That is the way the people live. There is no law, no shame, and no honor. Many of the young girls have children when they are only fourteen or fifteen years old.

"We also visited the hospitals. . . . It is not easy for the sick that are not of the Catholic faith. The nurses are all nuns; and the priests, who come often to visit, do not look favorably on those who do not kiss the cross and take part in all the Catholic ceremonies.

"We have a good school in Miraflores and although I cannot speak or understand much Spanish, I felt inspired by associating with this enthusiastic group of young people.

"After three months in Lima we started on the long journey to Iquitos. As the boat service from Callao round through the Panama Canal, and via Brazil up the Amazon River, had been suspended, we had to make the dangerous trip by land over the Andes Mountains and through the jungle. Elder Stahl told about this overland route when he visited Denmark. It is called the 'Piches Trail.'

"First we had to travel for eight days by train, bus, and muleback to get to our mission station in Metraro, where we should stay for some time.

"The train which would take us over the 16,400-foot Mount Ticlio pass left Lima at seven o'clock in the morning. It is the highest railway in the world. For some time we had been praying for God's special protection on this trip and in full confidence in His promise we boarded the train.

"In the beginning the upgrade was not very steep. The railway followed the Rimac River up through the valley over the route the *conquistadores* and the *libertadores* had traveled. The scenery was magnificent. At each station wonderful fruits of the valley were offered for sale to the passengers: mangos, *guayabas, granadillas, chirimoyas, paltas* and fruits I don't remember.

"As the train snailed its way higher up through the canyon, the effect of the altitude became more noticeable. In places the ascent was so steep that the train had to back up for a distance and then steam forward again. It is said that there are forty-six such switchbacks on this railroad.

"Some of the passengers became sick. They had headache, vomiting, and nosebleed. It is called *soroche*—the mountain sickness or [high] altitude sickness. Some even had to receive oxygen. The railway always carries oxygen tanks for emergency. They tell me that during the history of the railway not a few have died on account of the altitude. The Lord helped all of us; none of us felt sick with *soroche*.

"Coming down again to a lower altitude after we passed the highest point, we arrived at La Oroya, the station of a great mining town, containing one of the world's biggest copper mines. There we stayed overnight and continued our trip by car, or rather by truck.

"It had been pretty bad on the train, but the truck was a lot worse. The road, just barely wide enough for the truck, had in many places a deep abyss on one side and a precipitous wall of rock on the other. The slightest carelessness on the part of the driver would take us over the cliff and into the canyon.

"Imagine an overloaded car, with eight persons and all their baggage, driven by a young man of only eighteen. It was frightening! Many black crosses along the road marked the places where a car had fallen into the abyss and where passengers had died hundreds of feet below. How good that we could trust in God—we knew that our lives were in the hands of the Almighty.

"The next day the road became so bad and narrow that it was impossible to go on by car; so we had to continue by horseback. We rested a day at a coffee plantation, the one Elder Stahl had mentioned several times in his talks at Skodsborg. The people at the plantation had been expecting us for a long time, and now they greeted us with joy.

"They served us a six-course dinner, with a servant attending each of us, and with fine dinner phonograph music. Each of us had a room for himself. What more could we ask? They drove us in their own car as far as the road permitted, and there our Indians met us with horses. We bade good-bye, mounted our horses, and soon our kind hosts were hidden from our view behind the tall trees of the forest.

"We rode slowly along the narrow path which wound through dense brush, sometimes up a steep hillside and sometimes down through deep chasms and across rivers and creeks. Nothing seemed to hinder our faithful horses. What a delightful ride! . . .

"As we neared the mission station we saw our Indian believers come out to welcome us, and when we reached the compound some two hundred natives were gathered to greet us. They thronged around our horses and with love and affection shook our hands in thankfulness because we had come. It touched our hearts. I could recognize many of the faces from pictures we had been shown in Denmark. Among these was the witch doctor Julio.

"We arrived at Metraro mission station on Friday, and that night we had a big meeting with testimonies in which the Indian believers thanked the Lord for the gospel. How wonderful to hear their heartfelt testimonies. As we sang and I played my violin, their joy was indescribable. They had never seen or heard a violin before.

"At this place we spent one month, a very pleasant time in a good climate. Every day many visitors came from other places, some from very far away. Elder Stahl helped them with their troubles, cured their sicknesses, and told them about Jesus and His love. I attended school every day, together with the natives, in order to learn to speak Spanish.

"One day a chief of one of the savage tribes came with his men. He stayed at the school and received instruction in the truth. He and his twenty men were baptized. He told us that they had built a school in their village, planted a garden, and prepared a place for the teacher. 'Many years we have been waiting,' he said. 'But now,' he added with sorrow in his voice, 'the landlords have burned the school building and taken the land into their possession.'

"There was silence when he had finished his story. The teacher or the missionary had waited too long in coming. Oh, that the Spirit of the Lord might move our people to give more liberally so that more teachers can be sent out before it is too late!

"When the chief had learned that we would be at Metraro, he and his men had set out to come and see us. At that time of year they were not able to travel by river, so they had risked their lives traveling overland in order to be with us and hear the gospel preached. What great love! For weeks these men had traveled and suffered hardships in order to reach the mission station, but no one could see regret on their happy faces. The chief said he had been asked to warn us that we would all be killed if we dared to come that way. We are not afraid though. When Brother Stahl gets his new motorboat, we shall go back and visit that place.

"The days at Metraro passed quickly, and soon the time came for us to continue our trip. Early one Monday morning our whole company gathered in the patio. In all, thirteen persons would make the trip to Iquitos. The Stahls had taken seven Indians to be with them as their own children. They had given them all the clothing they needed and promised them food and lodging. They were going to go to school in Iquitos to prepare themselves to be teachers. Everybody in Metraro gathered to say good-bye to us, and nearly all were moved to tears. They followed us a long way into the forest, and their last words were, 'Come again soon.'

"For nine days we traveled a tough and arduous road partly on horseback and partly on foot. It rained nearly all the time, and so the roads were soaked and terribly muddy. At places the horses waded in mud up to their bellies, and we were almost continually soaked to the skin with the rain. Constant riding tired us as well as the horses, so we often walked. A new pair of shoes and stockings wore out every day or two. Every morning we started about six o'clock and had to ride or walk all day without eating till six or seven at night.

"After each day's trip we came to a house. A 'hotel' they called it, just an old shack with openings instead of windows and doors. An ugly, dirty place. The meals were very expensive. So in order to save, only a few of us ate there or took a room. Wherever we could, we slept on the ground around a campfire, but sometimes when it rained too hard, we had to get under a roof. In the morning we would boil water over the campfire and eat bread—good bread that Sister Stahl had baked for the trip.

"Although it really was a hard trip, none of us complained. Even Sister Stahl stood it well.

"One afternoon, after having traveled from seven o'clock in the morning, we reached one of these so-called 'hotels' and found it had been abandoned. Apparently its owner had become tired of being lonesome and had left. Of course, we took the house in possession and had a good time. First we all went down to the river and had nice baths. Then we built a big campfire. Papa Stahl sat outside the door fixing his guns and equipment. Some boys picked fruit in the garden, and others went to bring water. But how were we to get food in this isolated place? Two of our faithful Indians went into the forest, hoping to find yucca, and after an hour they came back not only with yucca, but with some fish they had caught in the river. Yes, these jungle Indians are wonderful. Soon we had everything ready, and we had the best meal we had eaten for a long time.

"Finally we reached Pucalpa, at the great river Ucayali where big boats took passengers for Iquitos. The boats were unable to navigate, however, until there would be enough water in the river. And so we had to wait three days.

"The food on the riverboat became our great problem —meat and meat, and such as we could not eat. Brother Stahl explained to the captain that we did not eat certain kinds of meat. It made him quite angry, but his anger passed. And when he saw that we did not touch monkey meat or pork, he gave us more fruits and vegetables and once in a while chicken. Worst of all, we did not have any cabins. No, the only cabins were for the crew. Although we had paid a high price for our passage, we had to sleep on the deck.

"At every place we stopped and could go ashore, the people crowded around Elder Stahl. They all wanted a teacher. Many of them had already built a schoolhouse and were willing to sacrifice all they could in order to pay for a teacher. Even the big landowners and state employees offered Elder Stahl all the land he needed, if only he would send a teacher. How long will they have to wait?

"One evening while we sat, playing the guitar and singing, the boat stopped at a place where there seemed to be nobody in sight; but not ten minutes passed before the whole boat was overrun by people. They all seemed to know the Stahls.

"One young girl came straight to Mamma Stahl, gave her a good hug, and begged that she be allowed to go with us. For four months she had been waiting every day for us. She wanted to understand the gospel. 'And now when you go away,' she said, 'I have no more hope.' Sister Stahl tried to console her as best she could and promised that soon a teacher would be sent to teach her and her people.

"While on the boat I became sick with malaria, a terrible sickness. There is no place on the whole body where it does not hurt, and the fever runs very high. For five days I did not eat. Even with so high a temperature, I periodically felt intense chills. But now I am over it. I feel very well. I am glad I have had this experience, because I can now better sympathize with those who suffer with this sickness.

"When I think of all these natives that have accepted the gospel of salvation, and of all those who are burning with a longing to learn more about Jesus, I send thanks up to God, who gave Brother and Sister Stahl the love to go out as missionaries.

"All these dear souls are the fruits of just two people who have consecrated their talents, strength, and means to the Lord. They show in their lives that they believe in the soon coming of Jesus and that the message is urgent.

"May their example speak to the hearts of many so that they will give themselves to the Lord with all they are and have. My thankfulness to God is great for all I have seen and heard and learned. With my loving greetings to all, Anna Jensen."

4

Pastor Stahl

Anna loved her work in the missionaries' home. She loved to visit with Mrs. Stahl and was inspired by her unselfish, loving, Christian life. In the Stahls' home reigned constant harmony and goodwill. She felt she could never have found a better school of preparation for her lifework. She wanted to be loved as they were, and she wanted to love as they did. To them there was no difference between native and foreigner, or Indian and white. Everyone enjoyed the hospitality and warmth of the home. How she enjoyed the morning and evening worships with the family! She felt that God was very near when the Scriptures were studied and prayers were offered. Sometimes when the family faced perplexing problems or difficulties, they would meet at noontime for special prayer, and how often they would experience peace and a knowledge that God had marvelously heard them. For example, the Stahls had to get their house and furniture sold before leaving for Iquitos.

"I will have to stay home this afternoon," said Elder Stahl after the prayers. "I must be here to attend the buyer when he comes."

Anna admired Papa Stahl. How characteristic for him to talk faith like that.

"How can you be so sure that a buyer will be coming?" asked Mrs. Stahl. "We have had the house up for sale for a whole month with nobody as much as showing an interest."

"God hears prayers. He knows we cannot go to Iquitos before we sell out. He will send a buyer, I am sure." Pastor Stahl stood up. "A lot of work has to be done before we are ready for the trip." Anna looked at his tall frame. He is as strong as his faith, she thought.

In the afternoon a sea captain came and looked at their things. I will buy all your furniture just as it is," he said, "and I am also interested in the house." He paid for nearly everything the Stahls had for sale. This relieved them of much worry, and although the purchase was not completed until later, they all felt sure that God had heard their prayers in a remarkable way.

Although Anna loved the company of the family, she sometimes felt a yearning to be alone. She would take her Bible and a writing pad and walk the three blocks to the sea cliff where she would sit in quiet meditation while looking over the great Pacific Ocean. She would read her Bible and write letters to her father and to Bent. One evening time had run from her. It had become almost dark before she returned. The sunset over the ocean had been most gorgeous, and she felt that God was very near to her. And now the walk by the gardens, under the lovely trees and across the Alameda—everything seemed to speak of God's love.

Pastor Stahl met her. "Where have you been so long,

Miss Jensen?" He seemed quite upset. "Mrs. Stahl is worried about you."

"Oh, I have had such a wonderful time of meditation and prayer at the cliff," Anna said. "I'm sorry. I did not realize it had gotten so late."

"You must promise never to do that again. You don't know this country. It is dangerous for a young girl to go out alone, especially with night coming on." He touched her shoulder. "I am glad nothing happened to you." They walked back together the last block to the home.

"I really have not gone out, have I? I just sat down by the sea wanting to be alone awhile to meditate." Anna knew that Pastor Stahl, as always, had only a real, fatherly concern for her. She felt sorry she had caused the family to worry. "I should have let you know where I had gone. I hope never again to cause you trouble."

Pastor Stahl was an honest, straight, and sincere man, a wholehearted Christian. He loved God and feared sin of any kind. His kindness and love for his fellowmen were so extraordinary that everyone knew it, and all who knew him loved him. Most remarkable seemed to be his ability to adapt himself to any circumstance or condition. Peruvian customs and foods were often strange to the missionaries. But he seemed to fit right into, and enjoy, those appropriate to the life of a Christian. He would visit the humblest hut with the same delight as visiting the richest home. And to the pleasure of his hostesses he would eat heartily of their native dishes, whether it be *chunos* (frozen potatoes), *chalona* (dried sheep meat), or highly seasoned *sopa a la criolla* (creole soup), or *papa a la huancaina* (potatoes from Huancayo).

In her room that evening Anna sat thinking a long time about how good Pastor and Mrs. Stahl had been to her and how much she had learned by being with them. She wished that her conscience had the same sensibility to right and wrong as theirs.

In Metraro

Anna had witnessed the Stahls' special gift of making friends even among the very rich and influential people in the capital and the wealthy landowners and ranchers in the country. But it was at the mission station at Metraro (now at Nevati, 50 miles northeast of Metraro), that she really saw how richly they were endowed with that all-important talent for a missionary—friendliness.

Pastor Stahl never tried to show himself as superior to the natives. He knew how to get right down to where he could reach them, where they could understand him. He would always greet the Indians with a great Latin American embrace, and often he would even lift them right off the ground in his strong arms and give them a good shake. They all seemed to really like that. The Stahls would enjoy the food the natives prepared and sit with them on the floor of their huts and converse with them about their families and their problems. On trips Pastor Stahl would follow the natives' advice about routes, etc., and he seemed to enjoy sleeping in their houses. He would visit the sick, pray for them, and do what he could to cure them. When they were in trouble, he would go to the authorities and try to get them out. And if he found he had an enemy, he would go out of his way to find that enemy to make him a friend.

Sometimes there would be enemies. Some in the Indian communities were afraid of the missionaries. The witch doctors especially did not like competition in their medicine work.

One evening a couple of Indians came in their canoe from a place upriver. All looked peaceful at the mission station. The sun would soon hide its orange face behind the tree-crowned skyline. The natives of the compound were just coming from their bamboo houses round about to meet with the missionaries for the evening worship at their small chapel. The visitors rushed toward the meeting place. "Where is the pastor?" they inquired.

"There he comes." Mrs. Stahl and Anna, who were on their way, pointed back to Pastor Stahl who was coming with the Bible and songbook under his arm.

"He wants to kill you, Señor Stahl. El chief Huari, he is coming tonight." The two men talked excitedly at the same time.

"How do you know? Who is Huari?" Pastor Stahl seemed undisturbed.

"He is a witch doctor. We heard him swear solemnly that he would kill you. The people of his village thought it would be better to kill you before you came than wait until your strange message and your miracle medicine reached their village."

"Oh well, we will have to go and talk to him. How do you know he is coming tonight?" The missionary looked in the direction of the setting sun and motioned toward the meeting place.

"We saw him come down the river. He has his canoe hidden not far from here."

"Good. We will go and see him after the worship." Anna marveled how he could be so calm. The two visitors went along to the meeting. "Be careful, pastor," one of them said. "He can be very dangerous."

At worship the missionary talked of the heavenly Father's tender and loving care for His children. "Be not afraid," he read from Jeremiah 1:8, "for I am with thee to deliver thee, saith the Lord." He asked God to protect him and to turn the chief Huari from his wicked intention.

"Let us go," he said to the mission boy after the meeting. Several of the villagers offered to go with him. Anna wondered how he dared go out in search of an enemy now that darkness was coming on.

Mrs. Stahl begged him not to go. "He will be on the watch for you and may hit you with one of his poison arrows. Please don't go now. You can wait till tomorrow."

"No," insisted her husband, "we must find this man before he goes ahead with his wicked act. He doesn't know any better. If we talk with him, we may save him and through him make friends with his people." He kissed his wife good-bye. "God will be with us," he said. Soon they were on their way. Anna noticed that he did not take his gun along, though he took a flashlight.

Anna and Mrs. Stahl waited anxiously together with their adopted Indian girl, Chavi. Hours passed with no sign of the men's return. What a long, long night of worry and anxiety, a sleepless night of watching and waiting and of many prayers. All night Pastor Stahl was gone, and not until broad daylight did the first messengers come with the good news that the men were on their way back.

"There they come!" The happy cry went all around the campground. Anna looked down the road leading to the river. There she could see the men coming. Pastor Stahl had his arm around the strange witch doctor. He seemed very happy.

"This is my wife. And this is Miss Jensen." Pastor Stahl presented the ladies. "And this is my new friend, chief Huari."

"How do you do?" Anna and Mrs. Stahl shook hands with the native.

"It has been a long night. It took us a good many hours of searching before we found chief Huari. He kept himself well hidden." At this point Huari smiled. "But we found him and we had a good talk with him."

"All night!" Anna could not help exclaiming.

"Yes, all night. But what a beautiful night with moonlight over the river and the trees! We sat on the riverbank and talked about our Creator and His love for man. Chief Huari showed himself very hostile to begin with. But the Spirit of the Lord worked mightily on his heart, and little by little he yielded. Now he has become a good friend of ours." Pastor Stahl held Huari tight with his right arm around him. "We are friends now, aren't we, Huari?"

Huari nodded with a broad smile.

Although the missionary had been without supper and had not slept all night he did not mind. He had won a friend. The enemy and would-be murderer had seen the Light and turned his heart to the One who is the Prince of Peace.

Chief Huari stayed a few days as a guest on the mission station and learned more about God and His will. Then he happily went back to his people to tell them what he had seen and learned at the Metraro mission.

Pastor Stahl was not a great and eloquent speaker, but he had a way of getting right into the hearts of his hearers. He told stories and experiences as no one else could. And by his simple talk he captured the attention of all. The Holy Spirit did it, Anna often thought. She remembered how her own heart had burned in her when Pastor Stahl had told his experiences at Skodsborg and at the school in Naerum. The Indians loved to hear him speak, and always gave good attention in his meetings, but one Sabbath morning at Metraro his hearers seemed to lose interest.

"Now, never mind what goes on out there," Pastor Stahl interrupted his sermon. "Please listen to me. I have something important to tell you." He was speaking in their small bamboo church. From the pulpit he could not look outside. But his listeners, most of them sitting on the floor, could. They tried for a while to give him their attention, but soon their eyes and minds seemed to be outside again.

"We are in worship, studying the Word of God. Please forget what goes on out there and listen," the pastor pleaded.

Then a good brother could take no more. He stood up. "Pastor," he said calmly, "your house is on fire."

If there was anyone that did not pay attention to the worship then, it was Pastor Stahl. He rushed out, and sure enough, a cloud of thick smoke poured out from his house. Everybody helped bring water to extinguish the fire and to save the furniture.

The mission boy, Julio, came out from the kitchen swinging a great kettle of soup in his hands. *"Salva la sopa! Salva la sopa!"* he cried with satisfaction. Poor fellow! He burned his fingers. But he saved the soup. Anna had to laugh, he looked so funny. The fire did not do much harm, and nothing was lost except part of the sermon.

Like any young girl Anna had her dreams about marriage, and she found in the sweet relationship between Elder and Mrs. Stahl an example of what she dreamed her own marriage might be. The Stahls loved each other with pure and undivided affection. It seemed they were on a continuous honeymoon. Separation from each other pained them. But the reunion after one of the missionary's trips in the field could best be described by the words joy and love. They would sit together and talk. Elder Stahl enjoyed telling everything he had experienced during his absence. Especially when he returned from board meetings at the headquarters in Lima, they would talk and laugh far into the night.

They both had a great sense of humor, a humor that was contagious, but only of good feelings. Mrs. Stahl was a good matchmaker. She enjoyed bringing young couples of the church together, choosing those she felt might bring most happiness for both. And Eldler Stahl enjoyed performing the marriage ceremonies.

"Speaking of weddings," said Mrs. Stahl one day to Anna as they sat in the shade, enjoying a fresh breeze coming from off the river, "let me tell you what we experienced at one ceremony.

"Listen. It was over there, just after we had built the church." Mrs. Stahl pointed toward the chapel. "It must have been the first wedding in the new chapel," she continued. "We had put a great deal of work into the preparation of the marriage of Justo and Pascuala. Pascuala had worked in our home as our maid and Justo lived close. He was the son of one of our good neighbors. Both came from the Campa tribe. They were very fine young people.

"We had the chapel decorated with flowers and everything ready for the ceremony. My husband had taken his place up front. Pascuala looked so neat and pretty in the new dress we had sewn for the occasion. With flowers in her hair, and carrying a bouquet of jungle orchids, she really looked beautiful—and very happy. Beside her in dark suit came her fiancé, Justo, grave and serious. Everybody looked back at them as they walked up the aisle. But then I saw it! Oh you should have seen it. What a sight! I almost choked as I tried to suppress an explosion in my throat."

"What?!" Anna asked.

"Oh, you can't imagine. I couldn't believe my eyes."

"What was it?" Anna shook with curiosity.

"The bride came barefooted. And the bridegroom came wearing my old bedroom slippers!" Mrs. Stahl laughed in her hearty way. "It was just impossible for me to keep from giggling. My husband whispered, 'Hush! This is a holy thing.' Oh, how I had to struggle to keep a straight face! To most of the congregation apparently it seemed all right. But, think of it, my old bedroom slippers knitted of colored yarn with fancy trimmings! Sometime before that I had thrown the slippers out, and Justo apparently had found them and kept them for this occasion."

In Iquitos

Although always a humble, down-to-earth man, Pastor Stahl was respected. He captured the Indians' admiration. They saw him as their helper, defender, and educator. He also had the respect of the civil authorities.

"You have to make yourself respected, " he often said, "not for your own sake, but for God's sake and for the sake of His cause." That was the secret of his dignity—his faith in God and his assurance that God had chosen him to be His ambassador and messenger. Tall and strong, he walked with dignity among the people. He never went hunting, yet he carried a gun big enough to be noticed by everyone as it stuck out from underneath his topcoat. He never fired a shot.

"They have more respect when they know I am armed," he used to say. And there is no doubt that in those days it had its importance. Many times his life had been threatened. And who knows how many times his life had been saved just because of his gun?

To find a suitable hall or theater for public meetings in Iquitos had not been easy. "I would rent you the theater," the owner finally agreed. "But I am afraid the prefect will not give you permission to hold meetings here."

"He will," Pastor Stahl assured. "I am sure he will."

However, at the prefect's office the missionary did not enjoy much consideration or courtesy.

"No," said the *comandante* (commander in the army and prefect of the department). "You can't hold meetings in the theater." The *comandante* had not been able to capture the popularity in the city that he had desired, and now he thought he could gain sympathy and show his authority by refusing to grant the Adventists a permit to hold their meetings.

"The topics that are going to be presented at these public meetings will be to a great cultural benefit for everyone, and I am sure many will appreciate them." The missionary made a friendly gesture and smiled at the commandant. "We would like to invite you also, *Señor Prefecto.*" As customary in the hot, tropical climate, all windows were open on both sides and out to the street. A great many people had gathered and were standing listening to what went on inside.

"We are not interested in the sectarian religion of the Adventists here in this city. We are Catholics." The commandant stood up, apparently anxious to demonstrate his authority. He looked at the *gringo* (foreign white man) who stood humbly before him.

"We have religious freedom in the Republic of Peru, you know, *Señor Prefecto.* I have the authority and the privilege to preach the Christian faith."

"What authority? Here I am the authority—and no one else! He put tremendous emphasis on his words and clapped his hand on his uniform. "When I say you can't hold public meetings in the theater, you can't. I hope you understand."

"My authority is from the Holy Bible, and my orders are from above." Pastor Stahl pointed upward, raising his arm so that his gun became clearly visible. "I am sorry, *mi comandante,* but I want to tell you that even if you do not give permission, there is one—a greater authority than you—who will, if it pleases Him."

The missionary took leave with dignity and stepped out of the prefect's office. Everybody thought for sure that the meetings were out. The Adventist believers were much disappointed, but the missionary continued to encourage them, assuring them that God would take care of everything.

Two days later an order came from Lima to have the prefect arrested. When the police came to capture him early in the morning, he fled in his pajamas through his bedroom window. The meetings were held with great success. God had honored the faith and courage of His servant.

7/25/2013 c/g

5

Anna in Amazon Country

Brother and Sister Bernabé Chávez met the Stahls and their thirteen-member company as they arrived on the riverboat at the port of Iquitos.

"You surely did well, Sister Stahl," said Brother Chávez in admiration. "Just think of it—a *señora gringa* to make the dangerous Piches Trail from Lima."

"Thanks to God," said Mrs. Stahl. "He gave me strength and courage. I even enjoyed it." Then she pointed to Anna. "And what do you think of this courageous young lady who accompanied me? Meet Miss Anna Jensen from Denmark."

Anna smiled and shook hands with Chávez. "It surely feels great to be here at last," she said.

Brother Bernabé Chávez, a very faithful and consecrated worker, had done a good job taking care of the newly established work in the city by the Amazon, and he had seventy persons ready for baptism.

The Stahls rented a large two-story house on the main

street of the city, and here Anna had her first real experience as a missionary. Besides her daily chores with the family—cleaning house, washing, ironing, etc.—she helped at the small clinic which Elder Stahl opened in one of the rooms. Many sick people came daily for help, some with ugly tropical sores and ulcers which she cleaned and bandaged. In a letter to her friends in Denmark, Anna wrote describing her experience.

"Dear Friends:

"Here in Iquitos we have about 200 members. We are happy to work for and with these dear sisters and brothers who are very faithful both in giving offerings and in coming to Sabbath School. We know of none who have failed to come to Sabbath School in the time we have been here. Many of them come a whole hour before we begin services and sit for hours listening before getting tired. We have over one hundred children in Sabbath School. Sunday evenings we have public meetings and some 2000 come to hear the message preached by Pastor Henry Westphal. (Henry and Barbara Westphal came to Iquitos a short time after Anna arrived with the Stahls. See Barbara's book, *Bride on the Amazon*.) Our little choir sings many of our beautiful hymns, and we also have music selections on the violin and organ. Between the meetings we go out and visit the homes of the interested. They are all impressed with the message which is new to them, but few have the courage to follow the truth.

"Most of the people here in Iquitos are very poor. They live in poor houses that have dirt floors and mud walls. They don't have and don't need much clothing, and their food is simple. Their main nutrition consists of yucca and rice; they seldom have bread. Many sicknesses are rampant among them because of malnutrition and lack of cleanliness. There is no help whatsoever for these poor, sick, unfortunate people, and many die young because of these circumstances. Among these people Mrs. Stahl and I are doing our best to help. Greater misery I have never seen. One day we were called to help a sick young girl. She had labored in pain to give birth to a child for four days and she had suffered intensely. The doctor would not help her unless she paid him 160 soles, and that much money the poor girl had never seen. We found her in a shack where three families lived in the same room. She lay on a few sacks on the floor and had no clean clothes for herself or for the child she expected. We hurried to send home for what we needed. We knelt in prayer, pleading to God for help and guidance; and after two hours of working desperately with her, the baby was born and the girl's life saved. Sister Stahl is an expert in this kind of work, and I am very thankful for all I have learned from her. I can now take care of many such cases by myself.

"The same day we were called to another patient in the same situation, but the young woman died before we arrived.

"One old man we visited had gangrene in one leg. The medicine man, a *curandero* or *quacksalver,* had been there and poured boiling-hot medicine over the wound. The poor man suffered intensely. We came too late to help him. He owned only the rags he had on. His wound, full of living maggots, smelled terrible. He died a few hours later.

" 'It is so often like that,' Sister Stahl sighed. 'They call us when it is too late.'

"Immorality is widespread. Most fifteen-year-old girls have children. Daily we have syphilis patients with big, offensive, open wounds. Many people have intercourse with their own relatives, and the results are disastrous. A woman killed her husband because he had intercourse with his own daughter. She killed them both in bed and took her own life afterward. They lived in an isolated place out in the jungle. When our brethren found them, the two skeletons were in the bed and the mother's corpse in a state of foul decay. And two other children, a girl of twelve and a boy seven, were starving and near death. The boy was out of his mind, and the girl completely dumb. She is with one of our sisters now, but the boy died a few months later.

"We have made trips up the river in a small canoe, and these are very interesting. We find there is a longing among the people to hear about Jesus, but many are scared of us because bad rumors have been spread concerning our work. Some of our Indian believers have been put in prison. Many of you will remember the interpreter Elder Stahl told about. She and her husband are in prison now, and they have gone through a terrible time of trouble. They told how they were forced to eat pork. A piece of wood was put between their teeth and the meat stuffed down their throats.

"It can only give us joy to see how these dear believers have not forsaken their faith in Jesus. Yes, dear sisters and brethren, my heart is burning with love for this work. All troubles and privations are forgotten. Really one does not feel them when one looks at these dear people who know life only from the shady side. Soon the Lord will come. How many will be saved because you and I have brought the message to them?

"Greetings from Peru, with love, Anna Jensen."

One Sabbath in church Anna sat with a young girl, Miss Julia Rojas, a newly baptized believer. She spoke English. They had just heard a stirring appeal from the church missionary leader about *Semana Grande* (Big Week), in which he urged everyone to go out and sell books and magazines.

"Why don't we two go together?" suggested Julia. In her first love for the Saviour she wanted to do her part.

"Fine, " said Anna. "I am ready. I would especially like to go with you. Where and when?"

"Let us go down river a little way. I have friends down that way. We can go Monday."

"What about a canoe? Isn't it dangerous? Can we two do the paddling?" Anna wondered.

"My brother has a good canoe. He will let us borrow it, and I will get a boy to do the paddling for us." Julia seemed very confident.

"But aren't there a lot of snakes and crocodiles?"

"Oh, yes, there are," Julia answered, "but we will be careful, and God will protect us, you know. We are going out in His work."

"I will have to ask Mamma Stahl for permission. If she says it's OK, I'll go."

Anna felt happy that cool morning when they paddled out on the great wide river. Getting out from under the dense forest felt good. She enjoyed the open view over the waters and the fresh comforting breeze.

Young Chavi, who did much of the cooking for the Stahl family, had provided them with fried paiche (river fish) and yucca for the trip. And Anna had secured plenty of literature to be sold or given away. Julia had engaged a young boy to do the paddling for them. He was only twelve, but he was big and strong, and he knew how to handle the canoe.

Anna enjoyed letting her hand go through the running cool water at the side of the canoe. "It really feels good to be out here on the water," she said.

"I hope it is all right here," Julia took a searching look

at the dark water, "but you be careful for piranha."

"Piranha! What is that?" Anna asked.

"A piranha is a small fish, a terrible meat eater. If you should fall into a school of them they might finish you up in no time. They are known to eat all the meat of a big animal in just a few minutes."

"Horrible!" Anna pulled her hand up in a hurry.

Julia laughed. "Yes, you had better be careful. One day our dog had the tip of his tongue bitten off by a piranha when drinking from the river."

They stopped at several houses as they went, visiting with the people and offering them literature. And in the afternoon they came to a plantation. Julia knew Herr Schultz, the owner, a kind, German gentleman. He showed them around his farm and industry, gave them a good meal and pleasant lodging, and encouraged his workers to buy literature from them. But best of all, Anna thought, he listened with interest to their testimonies about the Saviour's love and His soon return to earth.

After a good breakfast the following morning they were on their way again. They came to a place with a number of houses scattered over the bank. Although they had spotted crocodiles, and the boy had warned them about snakes, the two girls braved their way to every hut. To their glad surprise, the people seemed happy for their visit and willing to listen. Many bought their magazines and booklets.

Going from one bamboo house to another, at one point Anna stopped and grabbed Julia's arm. "Look! Look!" she exclaimed, "a snake! Come let's get away from it."

Julia did not seem excited. "It is a real live snake, all right," she said. "A very poisonous one too. But don't worry. We will just chase him away."

"Won't he attack us?" Anna sounded scared.

"No. Snakes are afraid of humans, you know." Julia swung her bag on its straps violently. "Get out of here you tempter of Eve!" And the serpent promptly disappeared in the grass.

Time flew. Before they knew it, it was time for the two girls to be on their way back. But paddling against the current made the going slow. Soon darkness covered them.

"We will have to hurry," said Julia. "It's dangerous out here after dark."

The boy paddled with all his might.

"You had better put on the boy's coat and hat so anybody out here will think you are a boy," Julia suggested.

"And what about you?" asked Anna.

"Oh, I will tie a handkerchief on my hair with a knot in each corner as the boys do. And let us try to talk only in a man's voice."

They arrived back late, but safe.

"You girls are crazy," said Julia's brother when they were home. "You should know better than to venture out all alone after dark."

"I know, I know," Julia admitted. "But time flew. The current slowed us down. Let's just be glad and thankful we're here in good shape."

"Yes," agreed Anna. "God has been with us. It has been a great trip."

6

Anna's Great Disappointment

"Ding, ding, ding." The bell rang three times.

That was the last bell. The small river steamer pulled out from the pier at Iquitos. Then came the long, deep blast from the steam whistle. Anna was off on the 4000-mile journey down the Amazon River on her way back to New York.

"You must stay in bed," her friends had told her, as they bade her farewell. But she could not stay in her cabin. Fever or no fever, she had to see her dear Papa and Mamma Stahl once more before she left.

"Good-bye, Anna!" her friends on shore chorused, "God be with you."

"Good-bye, Mamma Stahl. Good-bye, Papa Stahl. Good-bye, everybody!" Anna shouted. "And thanks for all you have done for me." Her voice was choked, and her handkerchief dabbed at her eyes. There were the Westphals, her dear friend Barbara, the William Schaefflers, the Chávezes, Segunda Diaz, Sister Yzquirda, and many others. She had learned to love them, and she knew they all loved her. She smiled and waved as best she could, but the tears kept blinding her sight. Soon they were all far-away. But not until her friends disappeared as a small spot in the green forest, did she stop waving her arm.

A sad, depressed feeling came over her. Was this the end of her great missionary adventure? This question plagued her. Had it all been a mistake? To her great disappointment she had been obliged to give up her mission experience with Elder and Mrs. Stahl. She had not been able to overcome her malarial fever. Although she would get better between the attacks and would go about her work with Mrs. Stahl, the ague would always come back, and she would become sicker each time. The Stahls did their very best for her and treated her with loving kindness. Also Henry and Barbara Westphal and the William Schaefflers—young missionaries who had come to Iquitos to work with Pastor Stahl in the newly established Upper Amazon Mission—were extremely kind to her. So were her many friends among the church members who often visited her in her tent, leaving small gifts of sympathy.

She had enjoyed so much the visitation work with Sister Stahl. She had been able to do her little part, playing her violin at the great public meetings of Elder Westphal. And the neighbors and friends of the mission loved her. But now she had become so sick she could hardly move. She had become almost deaf, and her memory had become so poor that she could not remember even the address of her own father.

Anna felt sure that most of her trouble resulted from too much quinine, at that time almost the only remedy known for malarial fever. The horrible sickness had depressed her so much that she even got to the point where she did not care if she should die. And then an awful thought plagued her. Had it been a mistake to go with Elder and Mrs. Stahl to South America?

Anna did not doubt that God had called her to be a missionary. But why, why didn't God heal her? She had put her trust in Him, and although she couldn't understand His ways, she knew they were always the best for her.

The Stahls had been such a comfort to her. They had encouraged her and had done their best for her. But finally, to their regret, they had to let her go. They had decided to send her back to the United States where in a good climate they hoped she would regain her health.

"You must accept God's way," Elder Stahl had said. "He is the only One who really knows what is the best for you." How comforting these words had been to her. She tried to accept them. She knew God loved her and that His way was best.

Anna inhaled the cool breeze caused by the moving steamer, now sailing in the middle of the wide Amazon. She had not felt cool for months, except for the terrible chills of malaria. Breathing deeply, she looked up in the blue sky over the endless jungle, and even in the midst of her great disappointment she thanked God for His mercy. Somehow she felt a great relief from the steamy hot climate and the gloomy forest that, because of her sickness, had depressed her so long.

"You had better go to your cabin Miss Jensen," a voice said behind her. "It is quite cool for you here and you really should rest in bed." Anna, deep in her thoughts, had almost forgotten everything around her. Now the boat physician, to whose care the Stahls had so fervently recommended her, stood beside her.

"I shall," she replied. "But this cool air really feels

good." She walked down the stairs and found her room. The doctor accompanied her.

"You know what has been your trouble," he said as she unlocked the door. "You did not take enough quinine." The doctor handed her a small box of capsules. "Here, take these. You must take plenty of quinine. It is the only way you can beat the ugly fever."

"Ugly fever! You said it, Doctor!" Anna suddenly realized how feverish and weak she really was. "I surely appreciate your helping me to get rid of it." But she had no desire for more quinine. When the doctor had gone, she sat on her bunk in front of the open porthole. She hated quinine. She had had enough, she thought. She looked at the box of capsules. No more quinine, she determined." What will help me is this fresh air and a change of climate." And, before she really knew what she had done, out the porthole went the box of capsules.

"Oh, what have I done?" she reflected. Her conscience began to bother her a little. But it all came out as her instinct had told her it would. In but a few days of rest and exercise in good fresh air, she felt much better; and when the boat reached the Atlantic Ocean, she felt well.

"Didn't I tell you, Miss Jensen? The quinine did the trick!" The doctor triumphed. "You are so much better now."

"You did, Doctor," Anna said. Of course she left out the part about what she actually did with the quinine capsules. "How thankful I am that I again can feel a little like myself."

As the days went by and her journey progressed, Anna continued to improve. Exciting stopovers at Belem in Brazil and Port of Spain in Trinidad gave new impetus to her spirits. But now other problems emerged. The weather got colder and colder. Soon she would be in New

York in November, having only a few flimsy dresses designed for the tropics. And she worried about what to do when she got to New York all alone, having no friends to meet her and no money.

"How much money do you have, Miss Jensen?" asked the captain. "You know you can't enter the United States unless you have at least $200."

"Oh! What can I do?" Anna exclaimed, "All I have is five dollars."

"That is what the law says, Miss Jensen. No immigrant is allowed in the United States with less than $200. You may have to stay at Ellis Island until your consul can make arrangements for you to be sent back to Denmark." The captain did not seem worried though. "I will see what I can do for you," he said.

Only eighteen months had passed since Anna first saw the skyscrapers of New York from the SS *Leviathan.* And now, from her tiny freighter she again beheld the Statue of Liberty. She remembered how stirred with emotion and great expectation she had felt among a thousand immigrants and with Mamma and Papa Stahl. But now the future seemed uncertain and dark. Even Bent, who had come to the United States to study, could not come to meet her. How lonely and lost she felt! What Anna did not know was that the Stahls had already informed the General Conference and the New York transportation agent about her coming and that her good captain had sent a telegram to Mr. Adolph Dorn about her arrival.

And so, to Anna's happy surprise, at her arrival in New York, Mr. Dorn and Miss Mabel Porter were at the pier to meet her. How relieved she felt at the sight of these friends from the mission's transportation office!

"Welcome to New York," Miss Porter said. "I want you to meet Mrs. Klusman and her daughter Freda. They are

Danish and they will be glad to help you out the first few days you are here."

Mrs. Klusman greeted Anna very kindly in Danish. How sweet it sounded to hear her mother tongue again. Her acquaintance with Mr. and Mrs. Klusman and their two daughters, Freda and Ketty, blossomed into a friendship that became one of the highlights in her life and memory. They received her as a daughter in their home. They bought her dresses for winter, new shoes, and a warm overcoat. How wonderfully God had cared for her!

Only four days after her arrival Miss Porter arranged for a good job for her at the great Montefiore Hospital. There she earned a good salary and had her own private room. In spite of her poor English and the unfamiliar nursing customs in America, she gained the confidence of her employer and the sympathy of her patients.

A short time after, she experienced her first Thanksgiving. Then came Christmas. What a joyous time she had with her new friends in the hospitable home which she now called her own. Bent had come to the United States, but was separated from her by 800 miles. He attended Emmanuel Missionary College (now Andrews University) in Michigan. She longed so much to see him, but the sixty-dollar train ticket—one way—made it impossible for them to meet. They would have to wait until spring or summer, when school would be out.

One day Miss Porter phoned Anna at the hospital. "The conference president [Elder C. B. Haynes] wants to talk to you," she said. "Could you go to the conference office and see him?"

"I shall be glad to." Anna could feel her heart beat. "I have the day off Wednesday. Then I shall go." She wondered how he knew about her and what he might have to say to her. On Wednesday she presented herself at the

Greater New York Conference office. She felt a little timid as she entered.

"We have heard about your courageous mission service in the home of Elder and Mrs. F. A. Stahl," Elder Haynes began. "We appreciate very much your love for missionary work and all that you have done to help Elder and Mrs. Stahl."

Anna smiled and nodded. "Thanks," she said. "I really haven't done anything worth speaking of."

"Now the General Conference has asked me to assist you with any needed financial help," Elder Haynes continued. "Is there anything we can do for you?"

"Oh, no. I am all right. I already have a good job in the Montefiore Hospital. Thanks be to God. He has been so good. I really don't need anything."

"That's the girl," he said. "We certainly appreciate that kind of spirit." Elder Haynes put his hand on her shoulder. "And now about the expenses of your trip home," he said. "Don't ever worry about that. The General Conference will take care of all that for you."

"How thankful I am for that!" Anna's voice expressed relief. "I have been worried about that. The mission certainly has been very good to me." Then she added, "Sometimes I wonder if my missionary experience has been a great mistake."

"No, don't feel that way, Miss Jensen. I am sure God has His hand in all this. You wait and see."

Elder Haynes's words assured her. She felt grateful.

Anna found it a real privilege to work at the great Jewish Montefiore Hospital. Her nurse's training records from Denmark had been accepted, and they hired her as a regular registered nurse. God had led and blessed her, Anna knew, and she could not thank Him enough for it. She enjoyed a room all to herself, earned a good salary, and had freedom to keep the Lord's Sabbath. Soon she gained many friends among the nurses. And the doctors seemed to like her. But she had a hard time with her English, especially when filling out a patient's chart or writing a report. All were kind and helpful to her, however. "I will spell it for you," a would-be helper would say, not realizing that having the word spelled for her made it even more confusing. One doctor, who helped her kindly, called her "Half-pint."

Anna loved her patients, and they reciprocated. She found joy and satisfaction in service with a smile for everyone. It pained her to notice, when the shift changed, that some of the nurses would promptly leave the ward no matter how many patients were clamoring for help and attention. Before Anna would retire from her turn on duty, she would stand in the middle of the ward and ask if anyone needed further help, and only if everyone was satisfied would she say: "Good night, everybody. Have a good night's rest." All the patients on her ward were either chronic or incurable cases.

Anna loved peaches, a fruit that as a child in her native country she had never tasted. She had only heard and read about the delicious fruit, and now she thought it must have been a fruit from the Garden of Eden. She especially liked the peach halves in sweet syrup served in the dining room. In those days peaches came in five-gallon cans for hospitals and restaurants. One day she saw one of the kitchen attendants about to throw out some of these good peaches.

"You are not going to throw out these wonderful peaches, are you?" she protested. "You can't do that!"

"Why not?" asked the attendant. "What else can I do with them? If you want them, you may have them."

"Thank you," said Anna. And she went to her room

with a great big bowl of delicious peach halves. For several days after that incident her friends at the hospital nicknamed her Peach; she enjoyed peaches to her heart's content.

One day she couldn't find her purse anywhere. In her excitement over her lost purse, she couldn't think of a better word than trunk, a word she knew from her travels. So she began to ask around: "Has anyone seen my small trunk?"

"Your trunk! I didn't know you had a trunk," said her close friend. Her friends had another good laugh at Anna's expense when they found out that she meant her handbag.

A very rich Jewish lady, Mrs. Asher, came several times to the hospital to visit a friend, one of the patients Anna attended. She became acquainted with Anna and liked her. One day she said, "Miss Jensen, wouldn't you like to come to my home and be a private nurse for my husband? He has had a stroke and is paralyzed on one side. You will, of course, have your regular time off, but it will be a twenty-four-hour job. You will have everything and a very good salary."

Anna, surprised, at first did not know what to say. But she felt that God had something wonderful for her.

"Let me think about it," she said. "I will call you tomorrow." She consulted with her Danish friends, the Klusmans, and with Mr. Dorn and Miss Porter.

"Sure, don't hesitate," they urged. "It is a great opportunity."

Soon after, Anna found herself in a luxurious apartment on Westend Avenue. She had a beautiful room and dined with the Ashers, who treated her as one of the family. Her patient, Mr. Asher, a multimillionaire and a perfect gentleman, treated her with courtesy and kindness. She enjoyed her work with the old gentleman and the family, but most of all she enjoyed the daily ride with Mr. Asher in his chauffered Cadillac through Central Park. On these rides Mr. Asher taught Anna many interesting things about the great city, and he made it a point in their conversation to correct her English and teach her. 7/25/2013 C/g

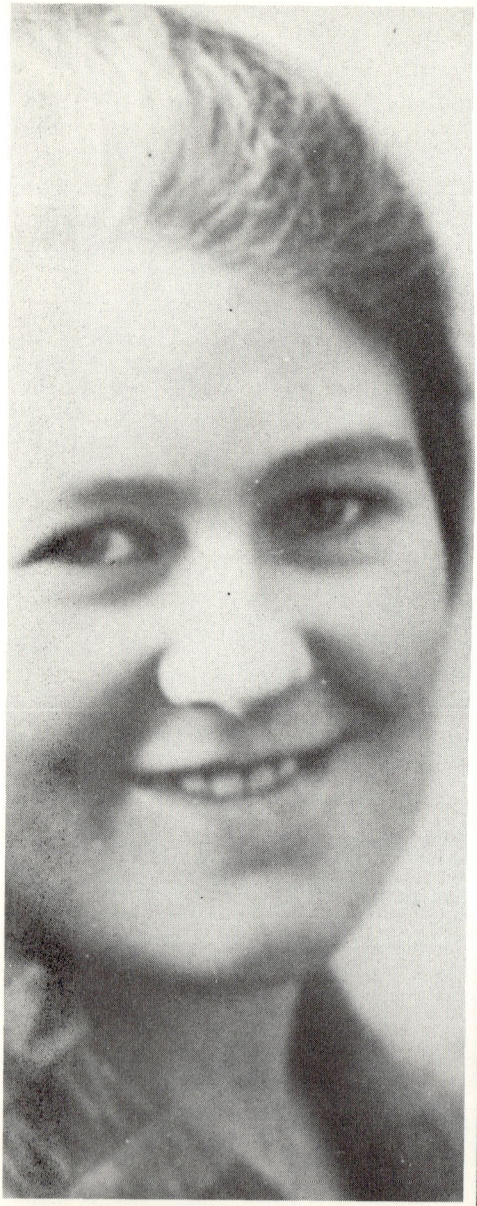

Anna in 1927, at age 27.

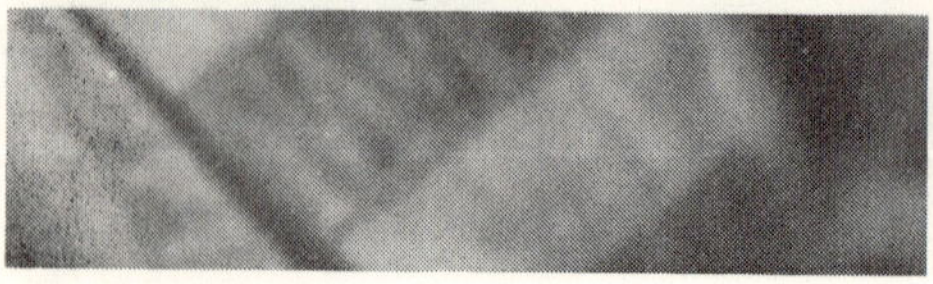

Skodsborg Sanitarium, "White City" in 1927.

Elder and Mrs. Fernando A. Stahl in 1

Mr. Adolph Dorn, transportation agent in New York; Miss Mabel Porter (now Mrs. Mabel F. Meister), Mr. Dorn's secretary; the Indian girl Chavi; Mrs. F. A. Stahl and Anna on SS *Esequibo* at departure from New York to Callao, Peru, in 1927.

A friendly church member near Tingo wants to give Anna a "burrito" (1929).

Broken Stone Mission Station in Umuchi near Moho, Peru.

Bent at a Chulpa or Inca grave on a mountaintop near Umuchi in 1930.

Mount Misti, Arequipa, Peru.

Dinner at chief Pedro Huanca's house in Umuchi in 1930.

The Broken Stone Mission family in 1930, dressed for the 28th of July, Peru's national day. Front row: Mrs. Bayllon, Bent, Anna, and Mrs. Ricky. Back row: Evangelist Bayllon, school teacher Castro, evangelist Lucchi and mission boy Ricky.

Chief Juan Condori, with his wife Juana in Umuchi in 1930, shows his tithe receipts.

Elder and Mrs. Fernando A. Stahl visit the Larsens at the Laro mission station in 1937

1262

Bent and Anna in 1934 on their first furlough.

Three delegates from the Urcos Mission Station at a missionary convention at the Juliaca training school, in 1939.

ent and Anna at residence in the Tingo Rest Home in 1938 while pastoring the church
Arequipa, Peru.

The three Indian Chiefs at Umuchi. Deacons: Mateo Mamani, Pedro Huanca, and Jose Condori.

Anna in 1950, at 50 years of age.

7

Anna and Bent in New York

After Anna had left Denmark and had been in Peru for nearly ten months, Bent and his best friend, Hans Rasmussen, said good-bye to their families and friends in their beloved Denmark and traveled to the United States. They crossed the Atlantic on the great Cunard liner SS *Lusitania* and began studies at Emmanuel Missionary College (E.M.C.) in Michigan.

They enjoyed their first Thanksgiving Day in their new country. Then, in just a few days, Christmas would come.

Hans stuck his head in the door as he passed Bent's room one day. "There is a big package for you in the post office at the store. It's from Anna Jensen."

"For me!" Bent jumped up. "A big package! What could that be? Come in, Hans. Wait for me here. I am going to get it right now." He hurried out. Soon he came back with a large cardboard package.

"Let's get this open! This is exciting!" he said as he cut

the string and ripped off the paper. "A box of candy! And what a box!"

"It's probably her Christmas gift for you," said Hans.

"Yes. Isn't she great?" Bent pulled out another box.

"Another box of chocolate candy! She really wants you to have a sweet Christmas." Hans smiled.

"A third box!" This time, fruitcake.

"It looks delicious. I will help you eat it." Hans informed Bent.

"Another! And another!" Bent dug out three more boxes.

"Six big boxes of goodies!" Hans threw up his hands. "Couldn't she have thought of something more appropriate for a Christmas gift?"

"That's the way Anna is, you know. When she gives, she gives generously."

"Yes, but look! She might have sent one or two regular-sized boxes of candy. But six like that! She must have a screw loose in her head."

"Well, she probably thinks I have friends here that I would like to share the goodies with," said Bent, trying to justify his sweetheart's generosity. But down in his heart he could not help wondering what ailed her. She certainly had overdone it this time.

Four boys from Denmark were studying at E.M.C. that year. A fifth Dane was a professor, C. M. Sorensen. Bent shared the delicacies with all of them.

Bent thought he knew English well. He could understand most of a sermon. But when the young people talked at the dinner table, they might just as well have spoken Chinese.

He could never forget his first day at E.M.C. when he walked around the campus feeling lost. Students would come up to him and talk. But when they found that he had not really understood what they said, and when they heard his broken English, they just turned and walked away. "What a discouraging feeling," he thought, "not to be able to understand."

Then all of a sudden Professor Sorensen came up and talked to him—in Danish. What a joy to hear the voice of his homeland!

A few days after the arrival of the generous Christmas package, a letter came from Anna. "I am sorry," she wrote, "that I did not have time to write a note the day I sent the candy boxes. I just sent them off without a word. You see," she explained, "I never accept tips from my patients. Most of the nurses do, although technically it is not allowed. And so, as my patients all know that I like sweets, every one of them gave me a box of candy for Christmas—thirty-seven of them!"

Only six of these she had sent to her sweetheart at Berrien Springs!

"She was not so badly off her head after all," remarked Hans. "In fact, she could have sent us more!"

During the school year Bent and Hans eventually learned to manage the English language. Although they had to work long hours from early morning, they were very grateful to the school administration for giving them the opportunity to earn their expenses.

When spring came and exams and the closing exercises were over, they separated—Hans for Tennessee and colporteur work, Bent for New York and Anna.

A couple of boys came to Bent. "How are you going to get to New York?" they wanted to know.

"Hitchhike, I guess." Bent shrugged. "Or maybe part of the way by train."

"Why don't we three buy a car and all of us go together?" one suggested.

"Buy a car?" The idea startled Bent.

"Not a new car, of course," they explained. "But we can get a small, good-running Ford for fifteen dollars. That is only five dollars each. And we can be going!"

"Great!" said Bent. "But five dollars! It seems fantastic to me, but I certainly am ready for that." He felt grateful to God for this wonderful opportunity to get to New York.

One of the boys had worked as a cook in the school kitchen. With his supervisor's permission he prepared a substantial provision of good sandwiches for the trip. The weather was excellent, and the trip in the beauty of early summer proved an unforgettable experience for Bent. They had only one mishap on the way—a flat tire. At Buffalo they stopped over to see the great Niagara Falls. At Albany, hometown of one of the boys, they parted—one for Boston, and Bent by train for New York.

Next morning Bent found his way down to the pier where the Hudson River boat would depart. By correspondance Anna and he had decided on meeting at that place. In the crisp, bright sunny morning Bent stood at the pier watching passengers as they came to board the old "glory boat" of the Hudson. He looked up and down the nearby streets to see if his sweet Anna would appear. A big black Cadillac pulled up right in front of him.

The chauffeur, a big, handsome black man in uniform, stepped out and opened the door for an elegant young lady. Bent took a step backward. He could hardly believe it! The young lady was Anna.

"Here I am," she said. "How are you, Bent?" Then she turned to the chauffeur, "Thank you, Anton."

Bent was really impressed. He had not expected to meet her just that way.

"She is quite a girl," said Anton as he drove away.

They enjoyed a scenic boat trip up the Hudson River in glorious June weather. As they talked, they made plans for the future. Anna earned forty-nine dollars a week, plus extra fees for massages and special duty. And she had been able to save most of her salary. She helped Bent to find employment where he earned thirty-five dollars a week—also as a private nurse. Eighty-four dollars a week for the two was a lot of money in 1929, and they had only few expenses for room and board. They were married that same month, June, and lived in a little apartment near Central Park. Their happiness lacked but one thing. They yearned to serve in the mission field.

In their correspondence with the secretary for missionary appointments, the General Conference had let them understand that they might expect a call to South America. However, as the summer passed no call came.

Then one day a call came through from the Inter-American Division. Brother Carl Christiansen from Denmark, a successful literature evangelist in Colombia, had suggested their names. And the Colombia-Venezuela Union had passed a call for them to work in Colombia as self-supporting literature evangelists.

It was not the call they had expected—self-supporting work in a strange country, and using a foreign language! How could they accept such a call, especially to a tropical climate like the one Anna had just been forced to leave? Yet the call had come to them through the Division and the General Conference, and they dared not consider it other than a call from God.

They put the decision off while they prayed more than a week. Then the time came when they had to give an answer. What a difficult decision! That day they would never forget. In the afternoon they knelt down in their small living room and in earnest prayer promised that if it was God's will they would be willing to go to Colombia. A sweet peace from God came over them. They kissed. Then came a knock on the door. A messenger delivered a telegram from Washington. Eagerly they opened and read it.

It was a call from the General Conference and the South American Division for them to go to the Lake Titicaca Mission in Peru!

"How wonderful is our God!" Anna exclaimed. That evening they felt happier than ever before. God had really called them to be missionaries in South America!

8

On to Peru

As Anna stood with Bent on the deck of the SS *Ebro* of the Pacific Steamship Company, her heart overflowed with sweet expectation and thanks to God. She knew that Bent felt the same way. She squeezed his arm as they contemplated the silhouettes of New York's skyscrapers, even more imposing with their thousands of lighted windows against the November sky.

"Oh, what a great day!" Anna said. "I can hardly believe it! My dream has come true. We are on our way!"

"*Our* dream has come true." Bent held her close. "We are together. God has called us. We are missionaries!"

"Did you notice how long my serpentine lasted?" Anna looked over the side of the ship. "I think I was the last of all the passengers to lose connection with friends at the pier. Wasn't it fun with those rolls of colored paper strips?"

"Yes, it was nice of the steward to bring them to us." Bent smiled. "Our friends really seemed to enjoy it. God has given us such dear friends, hasn't He!"

Anna stood thoughtful in silence, then said, "Look in there, deep in those crowded streets. People are rushing along, thinking only about money, pleasure, and clothes. Thank God," she sighed, "that we can leave this great, wicked city. How good God has been to us!"

"Yes," Bent agreed. "He could not have given us a better occupation for our lives."

That evening they felt the cold of winter. But two days later, when they sailed along Florida's brilliant coast, they felt the warmth of summer. To the passengers' delight, the stewards put up a swimming pool on deck for their pleasure. The four days before arriving in Cuba passed quickly. The many activities, entertainments, and meals which occupy the days on a passenger boat made the hours fly. They had their meals at the ship doctor's table. Accordingly much of the conversation concerned the question of diet. The doctor insisted that meat was necessary for good health. But there were plenty of good vegetables, and the cook did his best to substitute eggplant steak daily for meat on the menu.

"Look, Bennie! There is Havana!" Anna said excitedly. "Isn't that gorgeous?" The city rose in beauty over the blue water, its white buildings and green palm gardens shining in the sun. The famous old Morro Castle stood to their left as the *Ebro* entered the harbor.

They had barely landed when a group of local fellows crowded around them, wanting to guide them in sightseeing. The men all talked at the same time, pulling Anna to one side and Bent to another.

"*Ven conmigo* (come with me)," "*Ven aqui* (come here)," they said. Anna had to laugh. She looked at her husband.

"There is nothing else we can do," he said. "Let's go with this man." And soon they found themselves seated in an old open car with a friendly little Cuban who triumphantly and enthusiastically drove away with them right under the noses of his colleagues. Havana boasted many beautiful tropical flower gardens, magnificent royal palms, romantic old castles and churches rich with art and customs and history, and lovely plazas adorned by monuments and statues. For several miles they drove on wide boulevards with beautiful flower beds, but also through the old city with streets in some places so narrow that the iron balconies over their heads on opposite sides almost touched one another. In one of these streets it happened that the old car stopped! There was, of course, no room for passing. So the street became blocked.

"What do we do now?" Anna's voice was drowned in the tooting of horns from behind.

"We had better get out and walk," Bent suggested.

"No! No!" shouted their chauffeur. "*Tranquilanse, paciencia!* (Be tranquil and have patience!)." He seemed to be accustomed to this, for he called to the car behind and waved vigorously with both arms. A moment later they received a powerful push from behind. It sent the car bouncing forward. Another push and another and they were out of the narrow street. And by now the motor was running again, and away they sped, the happy driver smiling all over.

They would have liked to see many things in Havana. But time was short. They had to go back to the steamer. Two things, however, their Cuban guide insisted they should see. One was the home and gardens of the owner of a famous beer factory. Really fantastic! Enormous sums of money had been spent on this gorgeous home. The floors, for example, were laid with mother of pearl! In the middle of the garden was a fountain of beer for the guests. The second attraction he wanted them to see was a factory where the famous Havana cigars were made. But Bent and Anna had no interest in that.

Back on the boat, they sailed on to Panama. Each day it became warmer and warmer until, near Panama, they had to be on the upper deck to find relief. They arrived in Cristobal, Panama, at about seven o'clock in the evening. The boat was to stay there overnight, waiting its turn to go through the canal early next morning.

"Let us hurry with our supper tonight," Bent suggested.

"We certainly will." Anna seemed just as anxious as the rest of the passengers. No one seemed much interested in eating that evening. All appeared anxious to go ashore.

"How nice!" said Anna as she stepped into one of the small horse carriages that stood in a long row waiting at the landing. "It must have been raining. Everything seems so fresh, and the heat is not so bad. Doesn't it give you a strange feeling to be in a foreign country like this?" Anna looked up into the crowns of the majestic palms. "Everything is so interesting, so romantic, almost fairylike."

"Yes," agreed Bent. Even the air is different. "He drew a deep breath. "I smell the fragrance of eucalyptus and some kind of spicy tropical flowers."

"We are going along the old canal," their cab driver said, pointing with his whip to a building visible in the moonlight. "Over there you can see the old French hospital."

"Just think of it," said Bent. "That is where so many hundreds lost their lives in the hopeless struggle against malaria."

"Oh, please don't talk about malaria." Anna shuddered. "I always get chills when I think of it."

"It is interesting to think," Bent philosophized, "that here, just a few years ago, were jungle and poisonous swamps where Indians went around looking at the rusty machinery and other remains of the white man's failing struggle with nature. Now it's a healthy, modern city with all conveniences and sanitary features, where the mosquito is almost extinct."

Their friendly chauffer pointed out army and navy bases, the airport, radio transmitting towers, and, of course, the great Panama Canal, now a reality in spite of all the historical difficulties. He obliged them by showing them what they most wanted to see.

"We are Seventh-day Adventists," Anna said. "Do you know anything about them?"

"Oh yes, Madam. I certainly do." The driver turned his head and showed his white teeth in a wide smile. "They are nice people. I shall take you right to their church. Today is Wednesday. They are probably having their meeting right now."

Sure enough, when they got to the church, they found to their joy the prayer meeting was in progress. All the windows were open. They could see and hear everything. The meeting closed just at that time, and so they greeted the members as they came out. All were blacks. The pastor, a quiet little black man, gave them a good handshake and told them something about his church and the work in Panama. He also asked one of the young boys to take them to the conference president, whom they greeted in front of his little bungalow.

Next morning Anna woke early. "Hurry up, Bent," she called. "We must get up on the deck before the ship goes into the canal."

Even before six the *Ebro* pulled from the dock to begin the thirty-seven-mile voyage through the largest inland seaway in the world.

They watched the great water-lock gates as they

opened and closed. They marveled over how the great ship quickly and effortlessly rose thirty-six feet from the Atlantic Ocean in three steps, through three locks, to the level of Gatun Lake. Then three small locomotives on each side pulled the ship from one lock to the other. The honeymooners thoroughly enjoyed the day. Meals were served on deck while music played. After Gatun Lake they traveled the fifteen-mile stretch of the canal, and in the afternoon descended through two locks, first to Miraflores Lake and then to the level of the Pacific Ocean.

"Now we are heading for the equator," remarked Bent.

"Yes. Won't it be hot there!" Anna passed her hand over her forehead. "It felt hot in Panama. But what will it be at the equator?"

However, it got cold instead. One morning when they went up on deck they found that the swimming pool had been taken down.

"Why is that?" Anna asked the deck steward. "We are supposed to cross the hottest part of the earth, and now you take the swimming pool down?"

The steward smiled. "You see, Mrs. Larsen," he said, "we are now entering the cold Humboldt stream which hits the coast of South America just about at this point. If it weren't for this cold stream in the ocean, South America's west coast would indeed be hot. Tomorrow at two o'clock we will be passing the equatorial line. You be sure and watch for it," he said, and his eyes twinkled.

"Oh, no you don't." Anna laughed. "I have been over it before, and the captain tried to fool us into looking for it through his telescope so that we could see the line in the ocean. But we knew there wasn't any. We had a lot of fun, though, with a girl who actually did look for it."

For days they looked at the bare sandy coast of Peru with the dreary mountains behind.

"That is where you are going to live," the ship's doctor teased. "It doesn't seem very inviting, does it?"

Anna agreed. But she didn't seem to mind. "I know I am going to like it there. Lima is a nice city, and I have been over the mountains. It is a great country."

The sky over Lima, the capital of Peru, is overcast most of the time, but the day Bent and Anna arrived they were welcomed by glorious, bright sunshine. They enjoyed the ride from Callao, the principal seaport, to Lima, "the City of Kings." They felt they could not spend much time sight-seeing. They must find the Adventist mission. And so, after they had looked around a short time in the beautiful city, admiring the president's palace, the famous old cathedral founded by Francisco Pizarro, and the archbishop's palace, they set out to find the Adventist headquarters. They found it in an interesting way.

At the post office, where they had gone to mail a letter, Anna suddenly pointed out a man. "See that man over there?" she said. "I believe he is an Adventist." She walked over to him and asked him in the little Spanish that she knew if he could tell her where to find the Adventist mission.

"Right here!" He said, pointing at himself. It was Pastor J. T. Thompsen, president of the Peru Mission.

Brother Thompsen could even speak Norwegian. So lively conversation and handshakes followed. At the mission conference office Pastor Thompsen introduced them to Pastor H. B. Lundquist, educational secretary of the Inca Union Mission. They also met Brother Gambetta and others. Everyone gave them a hearty welcome. "We have been waiting for you," they said.

A long ride by car took them by beautiful plazas, parks,

and even the old zoo. They arrived in Miraflores where the brethren lived and where the Inca Union Academy is located. Almost everything and everybody were familiar to Anna, from the time she lived there with the Stahls. The Thompsens invited them to their house for lunch, and they both felt really at home.

"How it reminded me of good old Naerum," said Bent after they had visited the school. "I felt the same spirit and the same enthusiasm for the Lord's work."

Anna echoed his thoughts. "It is incredible what can be accomplished with the help of these dedicated young people," she said.

"Yes indeed it is marvelous," added Bent. "Did you hear Principal [Dave E.] Lust say that the new girls' dormitory had been built entirely by the students?"

"And *la chacra* (the farm land), how nice and green everything looks in spite of the difficulty they have had with irrigation. Isn't it something! It never rains here in Lima."

When they again stood on the deck of the SS *Ebro* as it steamed off from Callao, they felt glad and encouraged.

"Hasn't it been a wonderful day for us!" said Anna as she looked back over the silhouette of the city. "Our first day in Peru!"

"It surely has," admitted Bent. "Nothing could have given us more courage and joy than to witness how God is blessing the missionaries."

Two days later they arrived at the port of Mollendo.

9

Broken Stone Mission

For Anna and Bent, disembarkation at Mollendo, called the "roughest port in the world," was unforgettable. Their good ship *Ebro* was anchored outside the small harbor while passengers as well as cargo were taken ashore in small boats. At the pier the passengers were hoisted from the boat by a crane. Dr. M. B. Graybill, from Clinica Adventista in Juliaca, vacationing with his wife in Mollendo, met them. He showed them how to get from the moving boat into the solid wooden chair which the crane swung up on dry land. The Danish consul, an Englishman, told them that they were the only Danish citizens in all southern Peru.

The train trip to Arequipa reminded them of a chapter from a fairy tale. At Tingo, Jacob Wagner, treasurer of the Lake Titicaca Mission, and his family met them and took them in to the town.

Anna stood on the balcony looking down into the patio of the old mission rest home in Tingo near the city of

Arequipa. The fresh, invigorating mountain air felt chilly but good. She warmed herself in the bright sunshine. The wisteria tree, which shaded the patio and reached the balcony, was in full bloom and the fragrance from the lovely blue flowers filled the air. She liked the little garden town of Tingo. It was a privilege for her and her husband to spend some time there while studying Spanish before taking up their duties at the Pomata Mission Station in the altiplano. The climate in Arequipa could only be described as excellent. Located near a volcano, Mount Misti, at an altitude of 7000 feet, it was a good place to become accustomed to a life in the high altitude.

The heavy door of the patio portal slammed shut. Bent had come from Arequipa. He appeared with a few letters in his hand. "Hello Anna girl! Here is a letter from Denmark. And one from the mission headquarters in Puno." As he reached the top of the stairs he said, "I guess we may just as well get accustomed to the native cooking fuel."

"Cooking fuel! What are you talking about?" Anna asked, surprised.

"Cow droppings, you know. That 's what they use."

"Cow manure!" Anna looked sternly at her husband. "You know we have discussed this many times. You have promised me, Bent, that I would never have to cook our food with such dirty stuff."

"Yes, yes, I know." Bent agreed and spread out his arms. "But we have a whole houseful of the stuff."

"A whole houseful!" Anna's voice sounded horrified.

"Yes, the Ruskers had to leave, you know. And they wanted to be sure they left plenty of fuel for us, so we would not get cold. They left the fuel shed filled to the top with dried cow dung for us. And the mission has already charged our account for the cost of it."

A few weeks later, Bent and Anna got word from Puno that the mission committee had voted to call them to the Umuchi Mission Station instead of to Pomata.

"What about the houseful of cow fuel?" Anna asked.

"Well, I guess we will just have to forget about it."

"Forget about it!"

"Yes. That is part of our missionary experience, I suppose." Bent shrugged. "But I understand that in Umuchi there is plenty of wood for burning. So you can be happy for that."

So Umuchi, the good old "Broken Stone Mission," became Bent and Anna's true destination and their first field of labor in the Lake Titicaca Mission.

The name "Broken Stone Mission" stems from the often-told experience of missionary F. A. Stahl with the Indian chief of Umuchi.

"Please send us a teacher," the chief, Pariapaza, had pleaded.

"I will," assured the missionary. "I promise. I will send a teacher for your people."

"But, Pastor, how will I know for sure that the teacher is the one that you have sent?"

Pastor Stahl picked up a stone, broke it in two, and gave one piece to the chief. "When the teacher comes," he said, "he will bring the other piece. If the pieces fit together you will know for sure that he is the one."

Pastor Stahl kept his word, and the chief received his teacher.

At that time, the best way to get to Umuchi was by boat. The mission owned a small launch called "La Paloma." But missionaries would often sail on the railway company's steamboat. Bent and Anna could never forget their first trip. They sailed on the small old ship *El Yapuro,* built in England before the Peruvian railway. It had sailed over the Atlantic Ocean, round Cape Horn, and up the Pacific coast to Mollendo. Here it had been taken apart and carried up piece by piece on muleback to Puno on the shore of Lake Titicaca. There it had been put together again to sail between Peru and Bolivia on the world's highest navigable lake.

It took two days to make the trip around the lake to the port of Moho, a few miles from Umuchi. So Bent and Anna had to sleep on board. Elder A. H. Field traveled with them. He and his family were located at Umuchi. But they had just been called to start a new mission station in Sandia, on the eastern side of the Andes.

On board the steamer were several men whom Elder Field knew. They seemed friendly, but when Brother Field began to answer questions about them, Anna became scared.

They were all guilty of assaults, robberies, fraud, cruelty to Indians, and some even of murder. It was discomfiting to Bent and Anna to think of such people as their new "hometown" neighbors. Though they did not know it at the time, these same people were going to be their friends. Later they even had them come to the mission station for a visit and really learned to love them. Even the priest on the boat became their friend.

The men noticed that the missionaries had quietly asked God's blessing before their meals. In the evening when they all sat around the table and alcoholic drinks had been served, one of the men suggested that the priest, like the missionaries, pronounce a blessing over *la copa* (the cup). The priest objected vigorously. But they insisted. Bent wondered. They were glad for their drinks. It probably never occurred to them that there was anything wrong with drinking. Shouldn't they be thankful? There would be something wrong if their priest wouldn't say grace. And in the end he did!

Pastor Field showed Bent and Anna the door to a cabin where a fellow missionary had prayed to God all night for help. The missionary had suffered greatly. He knew he had been poisoned by an enemy, and he dared not lie down to sleep. He had made an extreme effort to stay awake. He prayed continually till dawn for deliverance. In those early days of the mission work in the highland, a missionary's life was often in danger. But God's protection never failed.

Of all the mission stations of the Lake Titicaca Mission, Broken Stone enjoyed the most beautiful location. Its white painted buildings were nestled in a snug little valley at the base of a mountain bordered by a bay on the northern shore of the lake, surrounded by eucalyptus trees and fertile small fields worked by friendly Indian neighbors.

The missionaries had a convenient landing place for the mission launch not far from the mission station. So they often had the privilege of receiving visitors from the headquarters in Puno. Some things Anna and Bent brought with them came on the launch, but most came later on the lake steamer and had to be hauled to Umuchi on muleback.

In a month they were settled in their new home, happy and comfortable in their two-bedroom adobe house. Their furniture suffered in the transportation. One leg of their new iron bedstead was broken off.

Pastor Field, founder and builder of the Broken Stone Mission, and his family stayed at the mission with Bent and Anna for about a month before leaving for Sandia, initiating them in the work and counseling them for the future.

The mission's church was a large hall with dirt floor

and a corrugated iron roof. Inside were adobe benches along the walls and a spacious platform. A schoolhouse, a small medical dispensary, and a house for the evangelist and one for the mission interpreter completed the mission station compound.

The twenty Sabbath Schools of Umuchi had over a thousand baptized members. That first year they had to oversee nine schools. So Bent and Anna had plenty to take care of.

10

Exciting Day at Umuchi

Using a crude hammer, young Brother Ricky, the mission boy at the Broken Stone Mission pounded the "church bell"—a two-foot piece of rail hanging on a wire. The sound, like a bell, rang clear and strong to every corner of the Umuchi valley. It was seven o'clock in the morning. Time for prayer meeting!

Wednesday prayer meeting at seven o'clock in the morning? Yes—church members and friends of Umuchi attended midweek prayer meeting in the morning rather than in the evening when darkeness made it inconvenient. At sunrise, in the freshness of the morning, from every household of the mission station singing of hymns could be heard, indicating that family worship was in progress. But on Wednesday morning the faithful believers gathered at the church.

"Isn't it really amazing!" exclaimed Bent as he and Anna walked over to the backdoor of the church building. "All these dear people gladly interrupt their daily routine to come from near and far to sing and listen to the Word of God on a cold morning."

"It is the work of the Holy Spirit," said Anna.

As usual, Anna had several visitors after the morning meeting. Sisters and brothers brought her eggs, milk, potatoes, and other products which she would purchase. Then they would sit on her kitchen floor and enjoy one of Anna's home-baked buns or a bowl of soup.

"We are going to have fried cream cheese for lunch," said Anna one day when Bent came back to the warm kitchen. "Ursula has brought us some good cheese."

"Wonderful! I could eat some right now for breakfast." Bent warmed his hands over the cookstove.

"Along with the cheese-fry we will have *occas* (tasty potato-like roots)."

"I hope the old horse hasn't eaten them all!" commented Bent.

"*Ay, ay, que cosa* (what thing)!" gasped Juana, the maid, as she jumped up and rushed to the door. "That crazy horse!" she cried. "He's eating *las occas*!"

Las occas taste best when they have been exposed to the sun a few hours. And so Juana had put a tray of the precious roots on top of the wall, thinking they were out of the horse's reach. But by stretching his neck, the crafty old horse had helped himself to the goodies.

Bent had just sat down at the breakfast table when an excited knock on the door signaled an emergency.

"*Señor, tatai–tatai* (Mister daddy—daddy)! Please come to the home of old Antonio," the man at the door gasped, breathless. "He has been stabbed to death by a robber! *Tatai–tatai,* please come!"

"I will come as soon as I can," said the missionary. Juana, back from chasing the horse, translated for him.

Bent hadn't yet finished his breakfast when the man

came back again, even more excited. "*Tatai! Tatai!* Please hurry and help old Antonio!"

"What is the great hurry?" asked Bent. "Didn't you say that Antonio had died?"

"Yes, yes, but he still lives—a little bit." Juana translated. "*Tatai! Tatai!* Please hurry."

Bent, who had been thinking about what to say to the mourners, now understood that it was a medical emergency. Grabbing his medicine bag, he rushed off with the messenger. "Please call Ricky and tell him to come with us," he told Juana.

Antonio, a man probably in his nineties, lay groaning in pain. Early, before dawn, he had fought with a chief who had tried to rob him. One side of his face had been cut open by a knife. Bent was the best medical help available. After a quick prayer with the relatives Bent gave the old man a novocain injection to reduce the pain, cleansed and sewed the gashed tissues together, and bandaged the wound.

"A man with a bad toothache is waiting for you at the dispensary," said Anna when Bent and Ricky returned. "And Nolberto is back. He may want some books."

At the dispensary the toothache sufferer complained loudly, "*Tatai! Tatai! Hacha cau* (It hurts)!" pointing to his mouth. Before long the tooth was out and the man relieved from his suffering. "*Gracias. Dios pagara sunqui!* (Thank you. God will pay.)" This he said with a grin and a two-handed thank you sign.

Nolberto, the colporteur, had been waiting outside. "Hello there, Nolberto," the missionary said. "I sure am glad to see you. I heard you were in jail."

"*Si Señor.* They beat me up. They dragged me to the police station. Then they demanded that I be locked up!"

"How could they do that? You didn't do anything

wrong, did you?" Bent quizzed him.

"No, Señor. I was selling books in Huancane. Suddenly the authorities accused me of selling perverse and unlawful literature. They let me keep my personal Bible and hymnbook, but they took all my other books: Four copies of *Por Sendas Extraviada (The Marked Bible),* eight of *San Lucas* (Luke's Gospel), and the rest of the Bibles.

"But then the police chief showed me real kindness. He told the commissary that Adventists were good people and that the books they sold were good books."

"And then he let you go?" Bent asked.

"No, Señor, he didn't. I guess he had to please the authorities."

"Oh, then he really did lock you up in jail?"

"Yes; I had to sleep at the police station. How glad I was I had my Bible! I read it and prayed much during the night. And would you believe it? In the morning he had my books ready for me!" Nolberto said triumphantly.

"He did?"

"God heard my prayers and worked it out. If the police chief had not kept me in jail, I wouldn't have gotten my books back." Nolberto held up his pile of books. "The police chief told me that he had demanded that the books be brought to him. If not, he would have to arrest the district governor for stealing! He said he knew the Adventists in Puno and had attended some meetings. He told me to be faithful in my work. Then he let me go."

"How wonderful a God we serve," thought Bent. "He certainly blesses our humble colporteurs."

Paperwork also had to be done at the mission station that day. A letter had to be written before Ricky went to town, and the church ledger had to be brought up to date. The evangelist had brought forty envelopes with tithe the day before; and although the amounts in each envelope were very small, they had to be faithfully entered in the books. One brother had given 20 cents, another 25 cents, another 10. One sister gave 15 cents, etc. It seemed so little. Yet, when one considered how little these dear church members earned by their labor and their produce in a week, it was reasonable tithe. Imagine what a blessed surprise to the missionaries that same afternoon when Chief Pedro Huanca came and handed them a Peruvian 100-sol bill.

"What is that for, Brother Huanca?" asked Bent in wonder. Even he had never seen a 100-sol bill.

"It is my tithe." Old chief Pedro looked at the two young missionaries. "It is for the Lord."

"But, Brother Huanca, you couldn't possibly have earned a thousand soles." Anna couldn't believe it.

"I know, *Señora* Anna. I have not actually earned a thousand soles. Yet I owe this to the Lord." They could sense the old chief's seriousness. "I have been thinking of your sermon last Sabbath, and I have been doing some calculations. I have thought of the value of all my sheep, my llamas, my donkeys, and of all the money I have lent out to different persons. It all comes to around a thousand soles, and I have never really paid tithe on all that. God has blessed me so much; I want Him to continue to bless me."

Other visitors came. A boy called for the pastor to visit his home. Bent always tried to take time for Bible study and sermon preparation. That day, however, both would have to wait till evening. Not all days were this exciting. But the missionaries' day was always filled with joyful service for the Master.

11

Field Trip on Horseback

Nothing is more stimulating and invigorating than early morning on the altiplano. This particular sunrise hour seemed especially life-giving. Anna felt good. She had worked hard to get everything ready. Now she relaxed as her good horse rocked her in the saddle over the stony road. How she enjoyed the gorgeous view of the Umuchi Valley, with mountains on one side and the green-reeded shore of Lake Titicaca on the other. She liked her work in and around the home at the mission station. But this trip was something else. Since she had no children to care for, she felt she could accompany her husband. And this was to be their first trip together.

Looking back, she could see the mission station. How nice it looked in the morning sun with its whitewashed buildings and its few eucalyptus trees. The mission boy and his family stood waving good-bye. Bent followed on his horse. "This is great!" she called over her shoulder to him. "I think this is the best part of missionary life."

"It is the toughest part, though," he responded. "We will get pretty tired. But the reward is great."

Evangelist Juan Apaza led the way. Their two dogs Lobo (wolf) and Rolly expressed their excitement by chasing back and forth and barking at each other while running between the horses.

"That warm sun really feels good." Anna let her rein down and rubbed her hands. "Every little cloud that blocks the sun makes me cold."

"Yes," said Bent. "Isn't it funny—my leg on the sunny side is hot, but the one in the shade is freezing!"

After a long and tiring ascent and an almost equally tiring descent they came to the little village of Moho, the nearest town to the Umuchi Mission Station. There they had to talk to the *gobernador,* a district authority who officially had requested the Adventist mission's brass band to play at a Catholic feast on a Sabbath day.

The young missionaries, with little experience and poor use of Spanish, felt somewhat timid as they entered the office of the *gobernador.* But he immediately made them feel at ease.

"I am most honored by your visit," he said. "We are here to serve you." To Anna he said, *"Sientase, Señorita"* (Sit down, little lady). He gestured toward an empty chair. To Bent, who stood respectfully with his hat in his hand, he said, *"Cubrese, Señor"* (Cover yourself, Sir)."

Bent had never heard that expression before, and so only succeeded in looking a bit confused.

"Cubrese!" the *gobernador* repeated, *"Cubrese!"* Then he smiled in understanding. "I mean put your hat on, Mr. Larsen. It's cold here. You don't have to take your hat off."

The *gobernador* really seemed most friendly and considerate. And it was not long before everything had been straightened out with mutually good understanding. And when he said, "*A sus ordenes* (At your service), Mr. Larsen," he really seemed to mean what he said. In spite of all the friendliness, the missionaries had been warned that they could not always trust the authorities. From the Bible, they learned to respect, obey, and pray for those in power. But they had to be on constant watch that neither they nor their fellow church members were placed in positions of having to disobey God. Some of the authorities became real friends of the missionaries and even visited them at the mission station. The town people needed the good news of salvation just as much as the rural Indians. And many times the mission was favored because of the friendship and sympathy of men in authority!

Next came a short visit to the mission school just beyond Moho. Then Bent and Anna were on their way over a mountain ridge, into a deep and cozy little valley, over a small river and up again. From the top of the next ridge they enjoyed a gorgeous view of Lake Titicaca, marvelously blue and adorned with many fjords and small, green islands. Beyond them they could see the valley far down below and the river over which they had passed about an hour ago. As Anna looked down the mule trail winding out and in between small fields, among Indian huts and a few eucalyptus trees, she wondered about the long distances. "Juan, tell me," she said, pointing, "way down there is where we shall go, isn't it? And when we are that far, how far will we still have to go?"

"Oh, we will have only two or three more mountain ridges to go over before we reach our destination."

"Not very encouraging," she thought. She already felt tired, but she did not lose her courage and still enjoyed the sunshine and the scenery.

In the middle of the day they rested in a snug corner between rocks where a small creek rippled by and where the grass grew lush and green for the horses. Their good lunch and a short rest on the grass gave them new strength to continue.

In the late afternoon they reached the place they had planned to visit that day. The people who knew about their visit came running from their houses to greet them and to accompany them to the meeting place. More and more people came until, by the time they reached the schoolhouse, they had collected a crowd.

At the school the local evangelist and the teacher met them, together with some of the most faithful church members.

Time had almost gone for that day, and they were tired. But after having shaken hands with everyone, they held a meeting in the schoolhouse. It felt good to witness the interest of these dear brothers and sisters in listening to the Word of God and the joy they showed for the Larsens' visit. They talked about their hope in Jesus, being faithful, and not getting tired on the way to heaven; then about the school and their problems. Bent and Anna helped them as best they could with counsel and encouragement.

"I am getting tired," said Anna at last. She spoke in Danish. "Let us not keep this on too long. I wish we could find a place to rest for the night."

This had already been arranged. One of the good brothers had prepared everything. Their "motel" was just an adobe house—one room with a raised adobe platform on one side for a bed. But how happy they were for it! The best blankets he and his neighbors owned were spread over the bed to make it warm and soft. While eating their evening meal they sat on one end of the bed and covered themselves with blankets. They were already shivering. They knew that there would be no heat and that the night would be extremely cold.

A simple meal had been prepared for them—soup made of potatoes and corn meal, eggs fried on both sides in lamb fat, boiled potatoes and *occas.* They peeled the potatoes and *occas* with their fingers and ate them with a little unrefined salt. They also tried their best to eat *chuños* but found them difficult to eat. *Chuños* are frozen potatoes, dry and leatherlike with a very peculiar taste. Brother Field had told Bent and Anna that *chuños* were good food and that they should never offend the Indian brethren by refusing them. Anna pretended that she ate them, but slipped them into the pockets of her leather coat. Being very hungry, Bent and Anna really enjoyed the good meal and almost ate too much.

After the meal they felt ready to crawl into their sleeping bags. But no, this was not allowed. Their friends were sitting round about on the floor looking at them. Others were coming. Soon they began to sing. Then they sang with great zeal and gusto. At first Bent and Anna joined with them in singing one good gospel song after another. Anna played her mouth-organ, sparking even greater enthusiasm. But after a while the already tired missionaries became exhausted and collapsed on the bed. Still their friends kept on singing until they found their guests asleep. Then one by one they stole away into the frigid night air.

Next morning Bent and Anna were on their way again, traveling to the school and village of Conima, the real destination of their trip. Conima Mission was new with only a few Adventists. But a school had been started there, and the people showed great interest. As Anna and Bent neared the school, they heard the sound of trumpets and saw people come hurrying from all sides. When the riders reached the school building, they found a large gathering. How glad all appeared to be for their visit. These new Indian friends squeezed their hands and said many, many things the missionaries did not understand but knew expressed thanks and satisfaction.

Inside the school building, the students were standing in two long rows. The missionaries entered. As Bent and Anna greeted them, they all answered in unison, their faces beaming. The visitors walked between the lines, shaking hands and expressing their joy at such a welcome. These were not Adventist children. They had been with the mission only a short time. Yet they looked washed, neat, and clean. Their teacher had taught them well. After the school had been inspected and the teacher congratulated for his good work, the students were given the rest of the day off. But they clustered around, very much interested in seeing what new material the missionaries had brought for their school.

On a small table, Bent and Anna unpacked schoolbooks, pencils, pens, notebooks, etc. Soon a sale began. Interest in everything ran high, but nothing received more interest than the free Bible pictures. There were joyful shouts as these were passed out to the dear children, who almost pulled the poor local evangelist to pieces.

Sick people also came, expecting to buy medicine and to be treated. This very interesting and satisfying work of treating the ill, once started, might well keep on all day. Everyone, sick or healthy, wanted a treatment or some medicine. If one had an eye infection and was treated with a dilute boric acid solution, everybody would want the same medicine used in his eyes. No small task it was to drip water into the eyes of fifty Indians, old and young. But they all felt better from it, so why not? Just to see the faces they made when treated and their smiles when the treatment was over gave rare satisfaction to the amateur ophthalmologists. Bent also pulled many teeth. As with the eye treatment, when one had a tooth pulled, suddenly a number of others remembered that they also had a bad tooth. Bent was not a dentist, but he really learned how to pull teeth. One day he pulled more than twenty-five teeth. Anesthesia was seldom necessary. When the tooth had come out, the patient would say, "*Gracias. Dios pagara sunqui, Tatai.* (Thank you. God will pay you, Daddy.)" They actually seemed to like the procedure. Often they would say, "Please pull another one." At first it was frightful to look into some of their mouths and see so many teeth rotten from the chewing of coca leaves. On one old grandpa the teeth were so loose and rotten that after Bent had pulled two with the forceps, he was able to pull out one more using only his fingers.

Anna cleaned ears with antiseptic solution and painted sore throats with dilute antiseptic. The people especially liked the pungent smell of spirit of sal ammoniac. "It helps for headache," they said. Many suffered from constipation and needed a strong purgative. Others came with diseases the missionaries could only hope to cure by prayer. Some came carrying the sick from long distances. Others had ugly wounds and ulcers. Some seemed to have tuberculosis or even cancer. Many of these the missionaries had to refer to the physician at the Clinica Adventista in Juliaca.

In the afternoon the work for the sick had to be interrupted for a meeting. The patients were told about the many terrible habits which caused their sicknesses. The gospel is power to save both soul and body. Nothing ever gave Bent and Anna more joy and satisfaction than to see the eagerness and joy of ignorant people, slowly accepting the light of the gospel truth, and little by little receiving the reward of a better life.

After the meeting Bent and Anna were invited to eat. Because of lack of time, no more could be done for the sick. After the good meal the teacher's wife had prepared for them, it was time to start back to their lodging.

On the return to Moho, the sky became overcast with heavy clouds. Soon it grew unusually dark. As fast as their horses could carry them, they rode over the mountain ridge. But before they could begin the descent on the other side, night fell. The evangelist had taken a shortcut on foot. So Bent and Anna had no one to help them find the way through the dark. Rain fell, then hail. Suddenly lightning struck very close and a roar of thunder burst overhead. Stunned by fear, the horses stopped and refused to take them any farther.

Getting off the horses, Anna and Bent led them down the steep path. Only during the lightning flashes could they see the path now and then. They had already given up finding the direct way to their friends' house. So they tried to follow the road which led through the village, hoping from there to find the way over to the school. As they silently rode through the small narrow street of the village, an unpleasant feeling overtook them. At this time a terrible revolution was raging in the land. Many horrible crimes, including murders, were taking place. They knew that behind these adobe walls lived some of the mission's bitterest enemies. In the continuing hail, freezing cold, and darkness they tried for more than an hour to find the little house of their lodging, but in vain. Bent's hands stiffened with cold until he could no long hold the flashlight. In hope of finding someone who would help, they knocked on doors at several houses. But at every place the answer was the same: "*Janihua hermano* (We are not brothers." After a long while they found the schoolhouse and the good Indian brother who soon guided them safely to a refuge. After a warm cup of herb tea they crawled into their sleeping bags. How thankful they felt toward their heavenly Father and to their native brother.

12

The Cross and the Stone Pile

When a highland Indian, crossing the Andes, reaches a high pass through the mountains, he will pause to rest beside his proud llama. At every pass is usually a cross of wood or stone. And beside the cross is a pile of stones, sometimes a large mound of them.

Often there are no other stones or rocks in the vicinity. One wonders where the stones came from. The Indian will tell you that travelers have brought them. An Indian will pick up a stone at the foot of the mountain, one perhaps weighing from two to ten pounds. He adds this to his regular burden, which often is already very heavy. But he carries both all the way to the top. There in front of the cross he rubs his legs, arms, and back with the stone, in the belief that some of his weariness will disappear. Then he drops the rock on the pile beside the cross, kneels, and worships the *Santa Cruz* (holy cross). Probably this is an old heathen custom including a Christian symbol.

How good is it to be able to tell the Indian not only about the true cross but also about the One who so loved the world that he gave His life upon a cross. How good it is to point out that salvation and freedom do not come by carrying heavy stones up the mountain trail, but only by faith in Him who bore our burdens on the cross on Calvary's mountain.

Many a time when passing a stone pile before such a cross, Bent and Anna thought of a spiritual lesson they might draw from this strange custom—when we lay our burdens down at the foot of the cross, we become free, and the weariness of sin departs. We lay our burdens down and take up the burden Jesus gives us—His yoke. When we carry a burden for Him and with Him, life's weariness disappears, and the journey is easier.

7/27/2013 C/g

13

Facing Death

"This way" was all old Brother Apaza had said as he met the missionaries at the outskirts of his village of Conima. Anna and Bent were very happy to see him and were about to greet him enthusiastically. But he placed his finger to his mouth, indicating silence. Something serious was taking place.

The missionaries had traveled all day from Umuchi, and it was just dark as they arrived in the little town of Conima. Silently Apaza led them, not through the streets, but by narrow passages behind *tapia* (walls) and over small fields to the back entrance of his home. He hurried their horses behind the adobe walls of his patio. Then, when they were safe behind the closed door of his little house, he uttered these words, "It is better that they do not know that you are here, Pastor," he said. "They might hurt you."

It was the evening before the opening day of school, and the missionaries had come to visit one of the best schools of the Broken Stone Mission Station. But a new public school had been established across the valley. And it was generally thought that there would now be no need for an Adventist school. However, as in former years our believers and friends of the mission had already registered their children in the mission school. The teacher had already arrived. By all means the Adventist school must carry on.

They heard a tramping of horses' hooves outside in the narrow alley. "There they go," Apaza said as he hurried out in the dark. A quarter of an hour later he came back and told of seeing the district governor and others, together with the public school teacher, leave in the direction of the new public school. In the flickering candlelight they saw deep concern in his weather-beaten face, and his voice trembled a little as he said gravely, "That is just what I feared. They are going to destroy our school."

That night Bent and Anna spent much time in prayer for their school, for the believers, and for God's work in that place. The missionaries trusted in God for help, and in their brethren and friends. But they knew that their faith would be put to a severe test. If God was with them—and they were sure He was—could anyone do anything against them? No. It was God's will that Adventist children should be in an Adventist school. Surely God would not permit it to be closed or destroyed.

The next morning, after many earnest prayers, the missionaries set out early to be at the school well before opening time. As they descended to the valley, from a distance they could see people gathering at both schools. On the road from both directions, as well as on foot paths leading to the Adventist school, the district governor had stationed men to prevent children and parents from reaching the school and to compel them to proceed to the new school. Crying children were being dragged to the public school. Adventist brethren were beaten. Some escaped and in a roundabout way over fields and stone fences managed to reach the mission school.

The men watching the road were much surprised when they saw the missionaries, who greeted them kindly but quickly rode by. At the school the parents and students and other church members rejoiced with renewed encouragement at Bent and Anna's arrival. Some cried, "They will come and destroy our school. They are going to kill us. They will take our children. We want a Christian school. We want an Adventist teacher. May God help us."

The missionaries were on the point of entering the schoolhouse when one of their Indian brothers came stumbling up. Blood was streaming down his face and all over his poncho. "Pastor," he said, "I made it!" Then he fainted in the arms of a fellow believer.

"This has gone too far," said Bent in indignation. "I must go and talk to the district authorities." He mounted his horse, and, although they all urged him to stay, he started on his way across the valley.

"Pastor, now they will kill you," they called. But nothing could stop him.

"If he is going, I am going also," Anna declared. Getting into her saddle, she followed Bent, trembling in fear.

Killing was not uncommon in that remote area only a few miles from the national border. Whenever a crime had been committed, the guilty person would cross the frontier and escape punishment. Other missionaries had been persecuted. Some Adventist believers had been put to death.

They found the district governor and the public school

teacher looking angry. As the missionaries approached, they stood in the path. On both sides stood ten or twelve men, each carrying a club in one hand and one or two large stones in the other. These stones, Bent and Anna soon understood, were intended for them. The missionaries dismounted at a courteous distance. Together they walked respectfully between the lines of glowering men. One of them hit Bent's sun helmet. Bent only smiled back. They stopped before the district governor and greeted him, then shook hands with him and the school teacher.

With Latin politeness the authorities accepted their greetings. One of the guards dropped his stones. Bent began to shake hands with everyone. Soon all the stones were dropped. The danger was over. The angels of the Lord had been with Bent and Anna that day, and by His grace had delivered them.

The missionaries appealed to the governor's sense of justice, talked to him about his great responsibility—the highest authority in the district—to preserve peace among all his people. He had done what he thought was right. But when he understood their point of view, he became very considerate. Complete understanding shortly came. They parted as friends. And both schools enjoyed an excellent year.

14

Warned By an Angel

In the old Broken Stone Mission dispensary, where the members' tithes and offerings were kept, was a chimney-like little room built in one corner. Only three feet square, it rose to a high ceiling. "What is that for?" Bent had asked when Elder H. C. Field showed him around the mission station. "It looks like a silo."

"That's just what it is," said Brother Field, "a salt silo."

"A salt silo! What for?"

"Well, you see, we have an important company of Adventist believers over in a place called Ñapa. They are all salt miners, and every year they bring the tithe of the salt they produce." Brother Field pointed to the open space above. "When the brethren bring their salt-tithe, we put it in at the top. I built it. It's handy for us. When we need to dispense the salt, we shovel it out from this chute at the bottom."

"Very interesting. I would like to go and visit the brethren at Ñapa," Bent said.

And so one day soon after the Fields had left to head up the new work in the Sandia valley, Bent said, "Let's go and visit Ñapa."

"Fine," said Anna. "I'm ready any day. I have heard about Ñapa. Such nice people. And I understand they have a school."

The next morning they were on their way by horseback. Up the steep ravine, over the great stretches of level terrain bordered by small Indian fields, around hills, and across icy creeks they went. The highland sun shone bright and warm, but the wind blew cold.

Anna seemed to be at her best. "Isn't this a glorious day," she shouted. "The scenery is gorgeous, and the visibility seems unlimited."

"The high altitude certainly has its special beauty," Bent shouted back. "But if it were not for the good sun—the 'poorman's coat'—we would be freezing."

The saddlebags were packed with their own necessities, medicine for the sick and books and other literature for those who could read.

Their interpreter, Juan, followed on his horse. "To the left," he said, when they arrived in the afternoon at the edge of a dry riverbed. The bed was about a quarter of a mile wide and covered with dry, cracked mud. It took an hour to reach a point upriver, where it had become narrow enough for them to cross over to the other side, and then another hour back to the point opposite from where they started out. Bent wondered often why they had not ridden right across the completely dry and seemingly hard riverbed. "Why is it that we did not cross the river right here?" he asked Juan.

"Oh, no." Juan shook his head. "It is not good that way. No good," was the best explanation they could get out of him.

They reached the school in Ñapa just before the students were dismissed for the day. So they had a chance to talk to them and their teacher and to carry out the usual inspection of the school. The students told their parents about the arrival of the missionaries and the scheduled meeting that evening. Bent and Anna spent a busy hour treating the sick and teaching the people. As always, they had great pleasure in meeting with new fellow believers.

The interesting thing about Ñapa was the salt mines which nearly all of the farmers had besides their regular fields. The mining consisted merely in leaching water from the salty soil and letting the resulting salt water evaporate. This they accomplished in small artificial lagoons. When the water had evaporated in the hot sun, a thin layer of salt remained. This they gathered and sold at the town's market.

The missionaries enjoyed a good meeting in the evening and the next morning started out early for Umuchi.

Since they had no meeting with the brethren that morning, they decided to have their own worship. After they had ridden for about an hour, Anna suggested, "The sun is getting warm now. Let's stop here and have our morning worship."

"Yes, let us do that." Bent swung himself off his horse. "This is a nice place. The horses can have a little rest too and some grass to eat."

That sparkling morning in God's nature inspired heightened adoration as they knelt among the stiff grass beside the icy-cold waters of a small brook. They felt God near in a new way. They prayed for His blessings over their faithful believers in Ñapa and for His protection on their return home.

Soon they reached the dried-out riverbed which the day before they had followed such a long distance on both sides in order to cross. Since they had left Juan behind at Ñapa to attend to the work there, they were riding back alone.

"Why can't we ride over the dry riverbed instead of making that two-hour detour?" Bent wondered.

"Don't you remember what Juan said yesterday? It is not good to go that way," protested Anna.

"But see how hard it is to ride on," Bent exclaimed, already far out on the firm, dry riverbed. "It is as good as a paved highway." How pleasant to ride on the smooth, stoneless ground. But it is strange, Bent thought to himself, that there are no footprints or animal tracks across the mud. Still he rode on, Anna following.

Near the middle Anna suddenly halted her horse and shouted, "Stop! Look!" She pointed to the far side. In the distance a man stood waving vigorously with both arms, evidently warning them not to ride farther.

Bent had scarcely reined his horse to a stop when one of its front legs sank down into the mud, almost pitching Bent over his head. Only with extreme effort in that terrifying moment was he able, very slowly, to extricate the poor animal's leg.

How thankful they felt when they turned and started back on solid ground!

"We must thank that good man," Anna said. "He saved our lives."

Bent also looked back, waving his hand in thanks. "But —he is not there! Nobody's there!"

The man had disappeared.

When they had made the detour and arrived back at the spot where the man had stood, they looked for him but could find no trace!

"Could it have been an angel?" Anna asked.

"It must have been!" said Bent reverently.

They stood for a while on the spot where the man had appeared and looked down over the wide riverbed.

"Oh how terrible!" Anna said, "I can't help thinking how awful it would have been if we, one or both of us, had sunk in that salty river of mud."

"God has been merciful to us." Bent bowed his head. "Let us pray and thank Him for deliverance," he said.

15

Last Day at Broken Stone Mission

With pencil and writing pad in hand, Bent sat on a steamer trunk leaning back against a large crate of furniture. He and Anna had been asked by the mission committee to move to a new station in Sandia Valley on the eastern slopes of the Andes. They had worked hard getting all their belongings packed in boxes, trunks, and suitcases. Now everything was ready to be carried by Indians about a thousand feet up to the highland road. Some of the brethren had already carried the first bundles and crates up the steep ravine to chief Pariapaza's house for storage until the missionaries' departure.

"*No hay caminoes, Señor* (There are no trucks running, Sir!)," the men said when they came back.

"Why not?"

"Revolution, *Señor*!" The brethren seemed very excited.

"Revolution!"

"*Si, Señor.*" The interpreter who had accompanied

them to the hill told them. They had heard that civil war had broken out. All traffic had been halted. This was later confirmed by a telegram from the mission headquarters in Puno.

Bent looked out the window over the spacious patio. He could see the homes of the mission station's native evangelist and the school teacher. The evangelist's wife was out in the sun washing clothes in a galvanized tub while her three children played around her. Over to his right Bent could see the church building with its characteristic tower. The eucalyptus trees never looked more beautiful against the blue sky. Far beyond the neighbor's *chacras* (fields) he caught a glimpse of the dark blue waters of Lake Titicaca. He felt he never loved this place more than now—when they had to leave it.

"What are you doing, sitting there?" asked Anna, just back from a visit to the neighbors.

"Oh, I just thought I would use the time writing a letter or a story to the home folks. There is not much we can do now but wait."

"Yes, you're right, Bent. But I hope we will get word soon that conditions have normalized so we can go." Anna dropped down on one of the boxes to rest.

"Lucky that the revolution did not come while we were on the road," said Bent.

"Wouldn't that have been terrible! Isn't it wonderful how kind our neighbors are too! Mrs. Mamani is bringing us a good pot of soup." Anna made the finger sign she had learned in Peru, which meant good eating.

After a lunch of Sister Mamani's good soup, Anna suggested, "Why don't we go out and visit our brethren once more?"

"Good idea," said Bent. "It may be our last chance—maybe our last day in good old Umuchi. What better way can we spend it than by farewell visits while we wait?"

They made a somewhat strenuous but delightful hike up through the valley to Chief Pedro Huanca's house. They thought it best to visit first the three village chiefs, now the three deacons of the mission church.

Umuchi, that snug little mountain area at the shore of Lake Titicaca, never seemed more cozy or more beautiful. The fertile rows of potatoes, the waving barley patches, the green *haba-chacras* (horsebean fields), the multitudes of wildflowers and blooming scrub along the narrow way charmed them anew. Even the shaggy, tangle-haired dogs who fiercely rushed at Bent and Anna from every house seemed less frightening.

Anna sat in Huanca's terrace patio. The view from there never failed to delight her. She leaned on a great stone table—one huge flat stone—and wondered where Pedro could have found a stone like that and how he and his friends ever brought it up and placed it in his patio. Over to one side, the chief stood talking to Bent. How she admired the grand man! A real Indian chief! His whole body, and especially the features of his face, revealed not only strength but Christian kindness.

"You were chief of the valley before you became a Christian," she said when the men came closer.

"Yes, *Señora* Anna. And I still am. But things are different now, thanks to God." Pedro smiled at her and sat down on the adobe bench opposite the stone table. "Before the gospel came, I led out in all the festivities—in the dances, in the drinking, and in the fights." Huanca showed his fist and stretched-out arm from under his poncho.

"I really knew how to fight, and everyone had respect for me. I was also the greatest sinner. My life was entirely heathen and worldly. For that I am now very much ashamed. At all weddings, funerals, and other important occasions I was a necessary and unfailing guest. At all these I performed the traditional ceremonies. All feared me and my rod. I shall show you my rod."

Chief Huanca stepped inside the door and came out with a heavy rod, richly adorned with hand-beaten silver. "This rod was the sign of my authority. But now my authority is in what God says in His Holy Bible." His face lit up. And his kind eyes testified for him.

"Now I am a Christian. Now I am thankful to God for what He has done and is doing for me. Believe me, *Señora*, it took a long and hard struggle to turn from my old life of sin and gain the victory over many bad habits. But God gave me power, and I obtained complete victory. I was the first in Umuchi to accept the message of salvation and to be baptized. Since then I have never tasted a drop of liquor. I have not danced. I have not chewed coca. I have not beaten my wife. The sins that I boasted of before are no more."

"And yet you have retained your position as chief," said Anna with admiration. "You are still the leader whom everyone respects and honors."

"Yes, thanks to God. Now, instead of leading out in the dances and in all the wickedness, I try to lead out in doing good. My great desire is by God's help to lead souls to Christ."

Anna knew how often Pedro Huanca had come to the mission station to buy Bibles and tracts. These he then went out and sold, at the same time teaching the people the Word of God.

In tithing he also became an example to his people. Ever since his baptism he had paid a faithful tithe on his earnings. But the year he heard a sermon on tithing he paid tithe on the value of all his land and possessions.

This had been a real sacrifice for the chief. But he wanted to be right with God.

"There is something great, something godly about this dear old chief-deacon," Anna thought. She respected him and looked up to him just as much as to any of the Lord's servants in her homeland. "In heaven," she thought, "Brother Huanca surely will 'shine as the stars for ever and ever.' " She felt she would gladly have given her whole life to win only one soul like him.

Bent interrupted his wife in her thoughts. "Do you remember *mucha patanca*?" he said as he let his hand go over the surface of the stone table.

"Do I remember?" Anna laughed. "I certainly do, and I will never forget." Then she laughed again. She remembered well the first time they were invited to Chief Huanca's house. Elder Archie Field, his wife, Mary, and their children, Rovilla and Hollis, were with them at that time. There were many guests, and the stone table was piled high with all kinds of good food. There were potatoes in many shapes and colors, *chuños* (the frozen and dehydrated potatoes), *occas, habas* (hard-boiled eggs), pancakes, corn, and, of course, various soups. More than twenty kinds! From each family represented, the mother had brought a pot of soup, and every one of the good sisters insisted that the pastor and his wife should have a bowlful.

"What shall I do?" Anna asked Sister Field. "I can't eat twenty bowls of soup."

"I can't either," said Mrs. Field smiling. "I just take a few spoonfuls of each, telling them how much I like it and how good it tastes. And then I just pass the plate on to someone down the line. They don't mind. They just want to know you have had a taste."

After the good meal Anna wanted to express her

thanks and satisfaction to Chief Huanca.

"What shall I say?" she asked Brother Field. At that time she knew very little Spanish and nothing of the Indian language of Aymara.

"You just go over to Don Pedro, shake his hands and say, '*Mucha patanca.*' "

"*Mucha patanca, mucha patanca,*" Anna repeated several times to be sure. Then she made her way over to where Chief Huanca sat. Shaking his hand vigorously she said, "*Mucha patanca.*"

Huanca's face spread in a great smile. He looked at Anna. Then he burst out laughing. He laughed and laughed. And those who sat near joined him in his big laugh.

Anna couldn't remember how she got back to her seat. But she realized she must have said something either very wrong or very funny or both. The Fields also laughed. Anna had told the chief: "I have a big stomach."

"You rascal." Anna made a threatening gesture toward Archie Field.

Yes, Anna remembered, and all three of them smiled as they thought of it.

"Well, I guess we had better be on our way to another visit," suggested Bent. So after a farewell prayer with the Huanca family, they started down the path for Jose Condori's house on another hillslope across the main roadway.

Jose Condori, an Umuchi deacon, provides a prime example of what the gospel can do to re-create human hearts. He had been thoroughly converted and then lived very close to God. His life had been a continuing miracle and testimony to all in Umuchi.

"Do you know, Bent," Anna said after they had had a very delightful, blessed, and spiritual visit, "I often long to be with Christian friends back home in Denmark, to be together with them, to study the Word of God, and to pray with them. But a visit with Jose and his good wife really satisfies some of this longing. We always talk about the Lord, about heaven and about our preparation to be there. I enjoy visiting with him just as much as if he were one of our friends or relatives in the homeland."

"You are so right," Bent agreed. "I feel the same way."

Anna thought of the many times they had visited Jose and his wife in their adobe house. Its cleanliness and order and the hospitality of its owners revealed the good that had entered his and his wife's hearts. On each visit Bent or Anna soon opened the Bible, and they with Jose and his wife experienced the most blessed moments together with their dear Saviour. Many times on their long trips to their substations they had met Brother Condori, usually on Friday evening when he arrived to spend the Sabbath with them. On Sabbath he spoke to the believers. And although he did not read or write, his sincere testimony had an even greater influence than the sermon.

They made other calls and greeted other friends on their way. Lastly, they visited their third deacon, Brother Mateo Mamani. He was their nearest neighbor and the "grandfather" of the entire mission. He was always in the midst of mission station activities, lending a helping hand and giving wise counsel.

"Do you remember the first visit of Pastor Fernando Stahl?" Anna, of course, knew he did. But she wanted to give him an opportunity to say something about the great missionary the old chief loved.

Old deacon Mamani's face lighted up. "I sure do, *Señora* Anna! I have been with the missionaries here in Umuchi right from the very beginning. In fact, the mission station is built on part of my land. Pastor Stahl—oh, what a great man he was! He came first right here to my house. And I saw him give the piece of the broken stone to Chief Pariapaza."

"And what about the other piece of the stone?" said Anna curiously.

"Oh, I really don't remember. But Pastor Stahl kept his promise. He sent us Pastor Field. And he built our mission station. We can never be thankful enough to Pastor Stahl and to Pastor Field. They have brought so much blessing to my people and to me."

"I understand that it was you who destroyed the *calvario* dancing place. It took a lot of courage, didn't it?" Anna looked up and pointed to the top of the mountain where the old dancing place once stood.

"Oh, yes, *Señora.* We used to go there on Catholic fiestas and drink *chicha* (corn beer) and dance all night. That is also where we made offerings to the spirits of the dead. But no more."

Mamani looked also in the direction of the mountaintop. "Many people were furious at me for destroying their *calvario.* They attempted several times to take my life. But God protected me. There has never been a *calvario* in Umuchi since."

Bent and Anna loved and honored good old deacon Mateo Mamani as did everyone at the Broken Stone Mission. Bent and Anna could not claim any part in the conversion of Pedro Huanca, Jose Condori, and Mateo Mamani. But they rejoiced in what God had done and gave glory to Him.

"Do you know, Bent?" Anna said thoughtfully as she stopped for a moment at the gate of the mission compound. "I feel very happy tonight. As we walked home from these wonderful visits, I thought of how marvelously God has guided our lives. What precious, valuable opportunities and experiencees God gave me with Elder and Mrs. Stahl! Today I have walked in their footsteps. I can never thank my Saviour enough. He even knew that my disappointment in Iquitos would be the best for me. And now God has fulfilled even my fondest missionary dreams. Yes, even more than I had ever dreamed."